# The Million-Dollar Rebuttal

DAVID WALTER

Copyright © 2019 David Walter

All rights reserved.

ISBN: 9781796209587

# DEDICATION

I dedicate this book to my Father, who always told me as a child that I could accomplish anything I set my mind to, and my Mother who intensely believed I would be a writer someday.

INFORMATION")

   B. "YOU WILL NEED TO SPEAK WITH SOMEONE ELSE"

   C. "BAD TIMING: CALL ME BACK"

13. HOW TO MAKE CALLBACKS

14. USING EMOTION EFFECTIVELY

15. A WORD OF CAUTION

16. MY TWO CENTS ON IMPLEMENTATION

A. DAVID'S RECOMMENDATIONS

The Million-Dollar Rebuttal

DAVID WALTER

"Man often becomes what he believes himself to be. If I keep on saying to myself that I cannot do a certain thing, it is possible that I may end by really becoming incapable of doing it. On the contrary, if I have the belief that I can do it, I shall surely acquire the capacity to do it even if I may not have it at the beginning."

-*Mahatma Gandhi*

DAVID WALTER

Preview

# ADOPT BIG CHANGE

If you want to get rich selling to prospects that don't have a need, you will have to adopt big change. Change is what allows you to create demand.

For example, I've worked for years with IT providers and managed service companies, which are in one of the fastest evolving industries around. From my experience, the big change that most IT providers (MSPs) need to adopt is moving to the cloud. I recommend **CloudJumper®**'s Cloud Workspace™. Many times I've used their services to help make IT companies rich, selling to prospects that didn't have any need!

DAVID WALTER

Preface

# COLD CALLING IS NOT DEAD

I have been hearing the mantra "cold calling is dead" for years.

The fear of rejection prevents most business owners from ever attempting to make cold calls. They worry about getting past the "gatekeepers": receptionists and others who frustrate attempts to reach decision makers.

There is also a misconception that cold-calling success can only come from putting many people on the phone for countless hours. "It's just a numbers game," they say.

In this book, however, we will show that cold calling, when done correctly, is a worthwhile endeavor for almost any size company. Once you learn the right way to make calls, you will know how to set appointments in a short amount of time—better quality appointments—all using a resource you already pay for: your phone.

I learned the secrets to setting phone appointments during my years running call centers for IT companies, and my sales training, particularly regarding appointment setting, helped these companies make millions.

It's time you learned these secrets.

In this book, I will teach you how to avoid having your message rejected by saying what you know people will agree with. After all, people often raise objections when they hear ideas they disagree with.

I have long held the belief that most companies (and individuals) don't stop and take into account all the resources they have at their disposal to accomplish their sales objectives. Therefore, too many businesses and sales professionals can fail at achieving their goals because they never capitalized on their assets.

One of the companies I helped generate revenue through sales appointments was SADA Systems Inc. I was able to get them started with new managed services contracts and project work that netted them millions. Now they have grown into one of the nation's largest resellers of Google applications, and Inc. Magazine ranked them #1732 with revenues in 2013 of $38.4M.

While I was assisting SADA Systems with telemarketing,

# The Million-Dollar Rebuttal

Microsoft kept trying to sell them on their direct mail program. However, the CEO of SADA Systems, Tony Safoian, replied to Microsoft that his cold-calling vendor was working just fine, and he gave the following testimonial: "David Walter was instrumental in getting SADA's managed services practice off the ground over a decade ago. With his novel approach to appointment setting, he helped create over $1 million in annual recurring revenue."

Another oft-cited reason for downplaying cold calling is that it involves countless hours on the phone, as in "you must kiss a lot of frogs to find a prince." While this is true with industry-standard telemarketing practices, it's not close to the truth when utilizing some of the counterintuitive techniques I recommend.

In this book, I will crack the common cold-calling mantra that "it's just a numbers game," which feeds the perception that cold calling is not a productive use of company resources. With my techniques, you will see that you can convert more contacts by making fewer calls in the correct manner.

The reality is that cold calling is one of the most cost-effective forms of marketing available to small and midsized companies. While other forms of marketing might be a little bit easier in terms of generating in-bound calls, the truth is that those methods will always cost more money and usually take much longer to implement.

Contemporary companies hold organic Internet marketing as a marketing panacea, but that strategy costs more and takes a lot longer to acquire actual sales leads. "Pay-per-click" may carry the potential for "instant" lead generation, but it can quickly bleed a small business dry of its marketing resources, and the rules for success can change quickly.

Ultimately, a company should pursue a comprehensive marketing approach when resources allow for it. But in this book, I will show you that, when implemented correctly, cold calling can generate far more leads in a much faster time frame at a much lower cost than any other marketing option. Cold calling has auxiliary benefits, too. If properly documented, cold calls can provide a cornucopia of data that can be utilized for market research.

If you run a company, telemarketing should always play an integral part in your customer acquisition strategy as it allows your sales and marketing team to be proactive. And if you're a salesperson, there is no other marketing tool at your disposal that can have a greater impact on your income more than simply picking up the phone and making some cold calls!

Introduction

# STEPPING ONTO THE PATH

The motivation for writing this book came while I was traveling on a family vacation and wound up sitting next to a very friendly passenger on my flight.

I happened to be reading Good to Great by Jim Collins on my Kindle, and when my battery ran out, I decided to strike up a conversation with my neighbor. At one point, he asked me what I had been reading, and after discussing some of the interesting points about Good to Great, I learned my new friend had an interest in sales and, as it turned out, he had just accepted a new position with an engineering firm that sold testing equipment.

My first impression of this guy was that he was a professional engineer, but when I asked him bluntly about his job, it turned out he was really a glorified appointment setter. That's when my eighteen years of appointment setting came gushing out, and before I knew it, I was revealing all my cold-calling secrets!

Something strange came over me. It felt like I was living a scene out of The Rime of the Ancient Mariner as I spun my tale about achieving my phenomenal cold-calling goals. One by one, I explained all the points now laid out in this book, and when I was finished, I was surprised to find my conversation partner had actually paid attention and asked several good follow-up questions. So we kept our discussion going until we exchanged formal goodbyes in the airport.

What struck me that day was how the story I dug up from nearly twenty years ago had resonated so profoundly with someone outside my industry. If my story could resonate with someone in the engineering profession, then surely it could resonate with anyone from any company who needed to meet with decision makers to sell their products and services.

Today, there still exist countless companies that rely on cold callers to set up their sales appointments and plenty of salespeople who still make their own cold calls to fill their pipeline. Most of these sales and marketing people use outdated methods that deliver few results. I know because I used these same methods when I worked in retail sales and credit card telemarketing.

However, when I took a job with a company offering an employee leasing service, I embarked on a journey that would transform me into an iconoclast who would disprove many of the old sales myths. My new awareness about cold calling set me on a hot streak for over six months, allowing me to set more appointments in less time than anyone had before thought humanly possible. It's a number so insane that it still causes jaws to drop in disbelief when I tell it, but it's true. During that period, I formed the habit of setting fifteen appointments with decision makers in one eight-hour shift!

Imagine if you or your organization could harness the power of such a system and set up a massive number of appointments in such a short period of time. Think of the results to your sales pipeline, and to your bottom line!

In the next few chapters, I will tell this story: the changes in my attitude, calling patterns, presentation, rebuttals, and closing techniques that enabled me to achieve the impossible.

Before working for the employee leasing service, I had been working for MBNA Bank, and it was this experience that helped me land my new job. The marketing director who interviewed me had previously been interviewed by MBNA Bank, and though he ended up taking the job at the PEO firm, he was blown away by MBNA's processes and people. When he learned I had worked at MBNA as one of their top agents, he hired me on the spot.

At the PEO firm, the manager's method of training was basically to have new hires spend the first week listening in on all the existing agents while they made calls. It was during that week that I made a keen observation. I noticed the agents had unofficially established a benchmark of success of setting just two appointments per day. Not only that, I witnessed many of the reps started slacking off once they hit that magic number.

Even though I had never done appointment setting before, after observing the competition that first week, it became clear to me that I could easily give a superior performance. I remember thinking at the time that it would be easy to set five appointments per day if I really set my mind to achieving that goal.

It wasn't long before I had trumped the two-a-day benchmark and was consistently setting about three or four appointments per day. Finally, after a few months, I broke the five-appointment barrier and thought I had really achieved the impossible. Occasionally, one of the other agents would get on a hot streak and come close, but only a few could ever really hit that golden number of five a day.

Soon after that, a new employee started setting five appointments per day a few days out of each week, but never for a solid week. That's when I decided to set my goal for an even more unthinkable number of fifteen appointments per day.

At the time, the number of appointments we could set was limited by the number of salespeople in each territory and, therefore, the number of sales meetings they were willing to take. Once a sales rep's calendar was booked up, the number of appointment slots for everybody else diminished. This scarcity triggered a race among the calling agents to be the first to book up the sales rep's calendar. If a calling agent wasn't first to book the sales rep's appointment slot, then that appointment was a lost opportunity. If I could set fifteen appointments, that would allow me to book the lion's share of all the available appointment slots, which in turn, would dramatically increase my income.

To guarantee I was mentally prepared to hit my new benchmark, I decided to implement a trick I had learned from See You At the Top by Zig Ziglar, which was to look in my mirror each morning and say my goal out loud: "I will set fifteen appointments today!"

Needless to say, the first day I tried this technique, the fifteen appointments didn't magically appear. (It would end up taking more than six months to achieve that magic number.) Nevertheless, I persisted with this practice of repeating my goal into the mirror every single morning. This was the first and most critical step needed to reach those crazy statistics because I would never be able to reach those numbers if I didn't first believe it was possible.

At the time, I didn't have any sort of strategy or plan other than just knowing exactly where I wanted to go and what the destination looked like. However, this process was effective in programming my thoughts and getting a message to my subconscious mind.

The human brain is a powerful supercomputer that,

ironically, has extremely poor communication skills. Generally, the communication process between the conscious mind and the subconscious mind is like putting a message in a bottle and throwing it into the sea in order to reach someone on a faraway island.

To ensure that even one bottle reaches its destination, you have to throw millions of bottles. This is precisely why people can't just instruct their subconscious mind to change with one command. You have to repeatedly, repeatedly, repeatedly send the message. This process of looking in the mirror and stating out loud that you're going to achieve an "insurmountable" goal not only helps you strengthen your belief, but helps send the message to your subconscious mind that you want it to come up with the solution.

Once the subconscious mind is triggered into action, all the incoming data gets processed through this filter. This process allows people to become aware and 'see' the things they need to do to fulfill their desires. A good example of this is when you buy a certain car and then become suddenly aware of all the other cars just like yours on the road. Once your subconscious mind is engaged, it allows you to meditate on the important questions in the process and get the answers.

It was this type of awareness that allowed me to solve the riddle of how to set fifteen appointments in one day. Over the next six months, I would get the answers to each question I asked and eventually solve all the steps in the process until I was finally able to fasten all the pieces together and make it work!

For anyone reading this book, if you truly want to achieve similar results, you're going to have to start by stating out loud your specific destination (i.e. the number of appointments you want to set or any specific goal you have in mind). You cannot skip any steps in the system. Just like a math equation, you must do this work in the proper order.

Even if you feel odd speaking out loud in the mirror each morning as you program yourself, just remember that most people who would judge you are themselves programmed by the world around them and not in charge of their own destiny. The good news is that, in your case, you don't have to wait like I did, hoping for the answers to come to you out of the blue. The answers are already written down, and to discover the secrets, you only need to turn the page!

Chapter 1

# HARNESS THE POWER OF YOUR SUBCONSCIOUS MIND

I first learned about the power of the subconscious mind while sitting with a friend who was a highly-motivated car salesman.

He had purchased a motivational series called Awaken the Giant Within by Tony Robbins. I had seen Tony Robbins's infomercials, but as of yet, his message hadn't resonated with me, at least not enough to trigger me to purchase his motivational system. Still, I was happy to get an invitation to listen to Tony's audiotapes with my new friend.

Later on, one of my business contacts suggested I read

Think and Grow Rich by Napoleon Hill, and it really opened my eyes to the true potential of the subconscious mind. After more time, I picked up a copy of See You at the Top by Zig Ziglar. That was the book that gave me the idea of looking in the mirror and reciting my goals.

Finally, one day by chance, I watched a TV news magazine segment (I believe it was 20/20, but I can't verify the source) where scientists were comparing the brain activity of ordinary people while they tried shooting at a target with an Olympic rifle. Researchers in white lab coats connected these people up to an EEG machine, measuring their brain waves. As anticipated, each of these inexperienced shooters had an explosion of brain activity while they aimed the rifle at the target.

Next, the host announced they were bringing in the USA Olympic shooting team to measure their brain activity and compare it with the novice results. Surprisingly, these experts registered almost no brain activity when they aimed and shot their rifles. As it turns out, this is the case for many professional athletes performing the complicated tasks of their respective sports.

While watching this show, I started thinking about everything I had learned about the subconscious mind, and it occurred to me that the complicated aiming process required such massive conscious brain activity on the part of the novices because they had no time to convert their thoughts into, what many coaches call, muscle memory.

I started to understand that converting a thought process into a habit meant that you no longer needed to consciously think about executing that process because it had already been converted into a subconscious thought pattern. In the case of the Olympic shooters, they really didn't have to think thoughts that could be measured by the EEG machine because their aiming process had been transferred into their subconscious mind. This process is much the same as switching on the autopilot on an airplane.

I remembered the many occasions where I had gotten into my car and then become deeply engrossed in thought as I meditated about some idea before realizing that, somehow, I had arrived at my old workplace instead of my current one. Somehow, my distracted driving allowed my subconscious mind to take over on autopilot, and it just drove to a common location I had driven to many times before. This last event showed me how the world around me had programmed my automatic actions, and it is what finally caused me to take action and begin programming my subconscious mind.

So how is all of this related to marketing success? It's not only important to tap into your subconscious mind to set your chief aims. It's also important to automate those skill sets like a finely tuned athlete.

If you only concentrate on consciously incorporating the techniques that follow in this book, you will always have hit-or-miss results. However, if you work on mastering each principle individually and meditate on implementing them one at a time, then you will successfully cement each technique into your subconscious. Once you have mastered all of them and continue meditating on them collectively, then you will have them all at your subconscious disposal at all times.

I can remember back when I was in the zone, setting all those appointments, and it felt like I was juggling these principles in the air simultaneously. The slogan, "Don't think, just do it," became my mantra as I abandoned my conscious struggle to execute and, instead, allowed my subconscious mind to take over. I was able to stop thinking about all the minutia and just let my subconscious mind put me on autopilot.

Ultimately, accepting this was the final step that allowed me to break through. I don't believe it's possible for anyone to break records without tapping into their subconscious mind.

Chapter 2

# HOW TO ESTABLISH A BELIEF

The only litmus test for evaluating if you truly have confidence in what you claim to believe is when you take action on those beliefs. Of course, this statement begs the question: "How can one firmly establish a belief so powerful that it enables action?" First, I will say that beliefs have to be supported with facts backed by concrete faith. I learned this lesson when I was trying to quit smoking as I kept telling myself that I believed it was possible for me to break the habit. After many failed attempts at quitting, I began to grapple with the very concept of belief itself. I sought a process where I could imprint my belief in such a way that it would finally propel me to take action once and for all to break my nasty habit.

This pursuit led me to the realization that I needed to relive all the times in my life when I hadn't been dependent on smoking a cigarette. I would close my eyes and meditate on different times in my childhood and play back each moment like scenes from a movie—riding the bus to school, playing with my friends, or going to a theme park—all done without desperately needing to smoke. After months of playing these memories over and over in my mind, I finally achieved a level of belief that I could finally live without smoking.

Harnessing the power of your subconscious mind is the key to producing the results you want in your personal and professional life. To be successful, you need to plant other ideas in your mind so they firmly take root and give you the confidence you need to reach your goals, and you need to meditate on the supporting "proof" that such things are possible. For me, the supporting proof came from replaying the times I hadn't been addicted to cigarettes, which proved to me it was possible to live without smoking. At other times in my life, like with setting appointments, the proof came from simply seeing someone else do it.

No doubt you probably said to yourself at one time or another, "If they can do it, I can do it." For many people, this one major piece of evidence is enough to produce instant belief! Once you have whatever points of proof you need, you simply need to repeat them to yourself over and over again, or take time to meditate on their reality.

You can claim these beliefs like I did when I stated my goal of setting fifteen appointments a day, but if you want to transfer these techniques and principles from normal conscious thought into the more powerful subconscious, then you need to develop a habit of repeating these concepts aloud, thinking about them over and over again and meditating on them.

When I wanted to change my thinking at the subconscious level about my desire to quit smoking, I made a list on a piece of paper of all the reasons why I should stop. I pulled this list out of my pocket and read it to myself every time I took a smoke break, which meant I was reading it six or seven times a day. I didn't relent on this practice for over a six-month period until I could tell it had altered my thought process.

First, I noticed how nasty the cigarettes started to taste when I smoked them. Not long after that, I set a quit date and finally beat that deadly monkey off my back. You can use the same process to achieve what you want by changing your thinking on a subconscious level. Start by making a list of your goals, principles you wish to adopt, habits you want to start, or even habits you wish to break.

Essentially, we are talking about brainwashing. You need to imprint or brainwash yourself with the changes you would like to make in your life. To assist you in this process, I suggest you read some of the other authors I have referenced, like Tony Robbins. Those resources with help you get a much deeper understanding of the nature of the subconscious mind, so you can successfully harness that power to book more appointments, close more sales, and ultimately make your dreams come true. And if none of that is sufficient in giving you that belief, just say to yourself, "If David was able to do it, then I can surely do it!"

Chapter 3

# THE "NUMBERS GAME" MYTH BUSTED?

When I set out to exceed my past success at setting appointments with decision makers, I quickly realized the key to closing more face-to-face meetings would be a dramatic upsurge in the number of contacts made each day.

Most companies and salespeople struggle with their ability to reach C-level contacts. The traditional view held by many call center managers, business development managers, and salespeople is that the key to making more contacts is simply a numbers game! In other words, reaching more decision makers is simply a matter of making more phone calls, or "dialing for dollars."

I have been hearing this mantra since my early days working in the call center at MBNA America, when my manager called me into his office to discuss what he referred to as my "low calling numbers." I was at the time one of the top members of the "pro team" that consistently won awards and collected the maximum commissions. Even so, I was still a little bit nervous while I sat there waiting to hear what my manager was going to say.

He started by bringing out data that showed my calling numbers were extremely low. He wanted to know what I had to say and was surprised when I admitted that the numbers were correct. He was shocked to hear me honestly admit to the low amount of calls. It seemed like my manager was about to begin a speech that would surely end with my termination.

However, just as the words were forming on his lips, I interrupted and asked if the calling data was the only thing he had considered, and I suggested we also pull up the number of credit card applications I had successfully closed. He agreed and began banging away on his keyboard, pulling up more of my statistics. After he pulled up all my data, he was shocked to find that I was getting more credit card applications than almost everyone else in his department!

Looking further, he also noticed that more of the people I submitted credit applications for actually used their cards compared to anyone else he had reviewed. He asked me to explain how this was possible. I told him that when you make more sales, you naturally spend more time with prospects on the phone, and therefore, less time dialing for prospects. Once I finished my explanation, he complimented me and sent me on my way.

It was this encounter that ultimately got me thinking that simply making more phone calls was not the answer, and in fact, the opposite might be true. And that led to a new question: could a salesperson actually dramatically increase their contacts while making fewer calls?

My next breakthrough happened while watching the movie The Pursuit of Happyness. I was captivated by Will Smith's performance as Chris Gardner, a San Francisco salesman trying to build a future, while taking care of his five-year-old son, despite nearly insurmountable obstacles.

While he was in an unpaid internship at Dean Witter Reynolds, he found it difficult to reach the top of his calling sheets each day. In the movie, you can see him looking at the prospects he hadn't yet reached and moving his hand up the list beyond the crossed-off prospects until he reaches the top of the list and decides to make that totally random, out-of-order call.

Suddenly, he hits pay dirt as this random call reaches the decision maker and lands him in a face-to-face meeting. It was the random nature of his actions that really struck a chord with me. It got me thinking about how the vast majority of cold callers or appointment setters work a list, how they simply start at one end and work their way through the list methodically. When you think about this pattern, it makes perfect sense as it allows you to easily keep track of the people you have already called, and after all, the order in which you call the list can't possibly make a difference, right?

Wrong. In almost every other endeavor in life, order is critical to a successful outcome. The example that immediately comes to mind is how critical order is in math problems because, if you tried to solve an equation in the wrong order, you would often be wrong.

It was then that I began to visualize what was happening inside the various companies that I was calling, remembering all the things gatekeepers would say when informing me the decision maker was not available. These statements ranged from, "He's in a meeting," to "They're out for lunch," and "She's at the bank." The reality of the world we are trying to break into is very dynamic.

It was then that I could see that placing one, single, solitary phone call into an organization with people moving around inside was almost a complete waste of time. The odds of reaching a decision maker by attempting only one phone call were ridiculously low.

That's when I came up with this strategy. If the person I was trying to reach in the morning had not made it in yet, then if I called back thirty minutes later, my chances of reaching them would dramatically increase. Following that logic, it quickly becomes apparent that the more calls you place to a business dramatically increases your chances of success.

Of course, like all things, there has to be a balance. Therefore, it's important not to make more than three or four phone calls to the same company in one day. You can keep this calling pattern for about three days, but after that, the phone screeners will begin to recognize your voice and start to associate you with an overly-persistent salesperson. This is why you should track your prospect down for several days and then lay off for about a week and then repeat the process all over again. I would say that you should only call through fifty names per day. Of course, as you call through the smaller lists, you will still make some "instant" contacts, but this is a natural bi-product of cold calling.

If you follow this strategy, the number of companies you attempt to reach each day will be lower than the average. However, if you continue to reach out to the contacts that were not available on your first pass, then you will make a breakthrough in your contact numbers. In fact, by following this strategy, you will start making fewer calls overall but end up reaching more decision makers. Don't we all want to get better results and work fewer hours?

Once you fully commit to this new "random" calling strategy, it's important to be prepared for the coming onslaught of contacts. In the following chapter, I will cover the challenge I faced when I hit my first gusher and share how I met that challenge. Later, I'll outline the steps I devised to convert the majority of those contacts into closed appointments. After all, you don't merely want to explode your contacts and just watch them go to waste because you don't know how to close. That's like leaving the cap off a gushing oil well.

Chapter 4

# YOU MUST BE ALL THINGS TO ALL PEOPLE

Once I disciplined myself to focus on tracking down decision makers with multiple calls per day, I soon had an explosion of contacts to deal with. However, instead of celebrating the sudden barrage of prospects, I was drowning in new objections—objections I had never crossed paths with before and marginal objections that in the past I had chosen to ignore.

It was extremely frustrating to have to file these solid contacts under "not interested" because I was not able to successfully convert them into closed appointments. What I had accomplished in the lead-generation business was comparable to finding the Holy Grail, but I wasn't able to bring it home. The pot of gold at the end of the rainbow eluded me.

After repeatedly running into these same obstacles, it finally dawned on me that the next phase of the sales process would have to undergo a metamorphosis, just like what I had done with securing more contacts. In short, my old techniques for handling objections would have to change.

I had grown comfortable relying on my old pat rebuttals, which had always worked in the past, when I only had to deal with a few contacts each day. But now I was facing an onslaught of new objections, and I was hearing more of the old marginal objections I had always ignored because they just didn't come up often enough. This compelled me to document all the possible objections and prepare an equally persuasive rebuttal for each one.

The company I worked for should have already mapped out these scenarios for their sales team, but they neglected to include such resources in our training materials. (Sadly, it's common to find this kind of lax attitude in management.)

Therefore, I undertook the massive project, myself, staying focused on it for about a month, which definitely bled into my personal time. The project allowed me to develop a comprehensive list of possible objections and rebuttals. Of course, this knowledge didn't magically get downloaded into my mind; instead, I had to practice going over all the rebuttals until I had mastered them all.

For example, I worked out how to handle the objections: "Employee leasing is too expensive," "We don't want to outsource payroll," "We don't want to give up control of our employees," and "Our employees don't need insurance." I even drafted a successful rebuttal for the dreaded "I have a friend in the business" objection.

When I analyzed the objections I received each day, I started to see a pattern. The objections seemed to come in groups of three. This meant I would encounter the same objection at least three to four times a day, and this was true for at least eight or nine of the objections. I found that if I made a passionate rebuttal for each instance, then I would be able to successfully close that contact, on average, two-thirds of the time. On some occasions, when I was really in the zone, I could knock all of them clean out of the park!

I knew the key to successfully dealing with my massive increase in contacts was to be prepared for every possible objection. However, I had not yet reached the point where I could convert twenty or thirty contacts into fifteen or more solid appointments a day.

I had already resolved two of the challenges blocking me from reaching the kind of paradigm shift in the appointment-setting process I so desired at the outset of my journey. But before I could attain my prize, I had to face an even more perplexing conundrum, and I'll be honest, that next barrier on my trek nearly caused me to throw in the towel. I will cover that story in the next chapter, along with the discovery that turned out to be the tipping point in the pursuit of my goal.

Chapter 5

# YOUR GREATEST WEAKNESS IS YOUR GREATEST STRENGTH

Initially, I was fairly heady with excitement from my success in tracking down more decision makers and getting them on the phone. From there, I learned to overcome objections by matching my persuasive rebuttals with their unique concerns. That was how and I was able to get these influencers to engage in much longer conversations.

However, this turned out to be both a blessing and a curse. These longer discussions gave me more opportunity to convert contacts into appointments, yet time and again, the majority of these prospects would still slip through my fingers. It almost seemed like I was in a Greek tragedy, the way I lost these sales opportunities that seemed so close to closing.

One day, the frustration brought me to my boiling point. I just couldn't keep my cool any longer, and in a moment of absolute aggravation, I threw my headset down and exploded from my cubicle. I took an extensive break, trying to find the light at the end of the tunnel. After all, I had come so far in enhancing the process. Surely I had to be close to a solution.

While meditating on where I had gotten in the process, it struck me that the majority of my calls were successfully transitioning through the introduction, questions, and conversation/pitch phase of the appointment setting process. Also, the lion's share of these prospects were even staying on the phone through the major objection phase. However, I kept losing them all at the same point: at their final request for me to send them information.

Even after I became aware of this annoying trend, its significance as the final piece to my puzzle still escaped me. I'm an avid chess player, and I pride myself on being able to think strategically. I would love to report that I quickly woke up to the reality that 60–70 percent of my dialogues were ending with the same objection, but I was stuck on this problem for a while.

My solution came when I one day recalled the following phrase from the Bible: "The weak things can be made strong." This idea got stuck in my head, and I morphed it into this mantra: weakness is strength.

Recently, I watched a documentary about the Maginot Line, the famous defensive wall France built after World War I to defend their border from Germany in case of any future invasion. The French really outdid themselves and built a virtually impregnable line of defense along their border, with one glaring exception. There was one area of their border France neglected because it was in a mountain region and nearly impassable.

However, when Germany invaded France at the beginning of World War II, they sized up France's defensive system and decided to attack at this point. How did this weakness make France stronger? The answer is it didn't because they hadn't meditated on the issue and determined how to capitalize on their greatest weakness. You see, if they had looked at their defensive strategy from the eyes of their enemies, they would have realized that any rational enemy would logically avoid committing suicide attacking their walls and would always gravitate toward undefended areas. If they had awakened to this rationale, they could have placed all their forces at their weakest point.

When you know what your weak spot is, you have foreknowledge and you can focus all your energy on that one spot. Since I was getting all my prospects to the point where they all requested information, all I had to do was devise the greatest "send information" rebuttal, and this would be the last piece to my puzzle. So creating the ultimate "send information" rebuttal was exactly what I set out to do, and it was so critical to my success that I now call it the Million-Dollar Rebuttal!

I stopped looking at the "send information" request as a negative and saw it for what it really was, a buying sign. After all, these decision makers could have just as easily said, "Not interested," or simply hung up the phone. The fact was that all the steps I had taken—qualifying, getting past the gatekeeper, dramatically increasing contacts, and matching up the rebuttals to their concerns—had aroused their curiosity, prompting the majority of them to say, "Send information."

In order to craft the perfect rebuttal, I began to meditate on all my past attempts to overcome this objection and analyze where I had gone wrong. Almost immediately, it was apparent that my negative attitude was being reflected in my tone of voice and coloring my entire approach. I could see that my first reaction to hearing that objection was to literally cringe and actually argue, trying to talk these people out of what they had asked for, and we all know from How to Win Friends and Influence People that you can never win an argument.

I knew I needed to make a 180-degree change in my attitude, start getting excited about hearing that objection, and let the prospects know that I would love to send them any information they wanted. Furthermore, I realized that I could take that positive reaction a step further by asking what kind of information they wanted me to send. This I predicted would blow their minds.

And I was right. Once I started making that response a

habit, I could sense these decision makers were utterly shocked that a telemarketer was taking their request seriously. Many of these C-level contacts would actually stutter when asked what kind of information they wanted because very few salespeople probably ever sounded positive about fulfilling such a request.

To my surprise, many of the prospects had to stop and think about what sort of information they wanted our company to send. Many times these hesitations would lead to several seconds of awkward silence. This is when I started to capitalize on predictable responses by "leading the witness" and making a few suggestions that would steer them into a closing situation, for example, "Would you like us to send references?" or "How about getting some numbers?" It was a little whimsical as nearly everybody would take the bait and say, "Yes, go ahead and send over a proposal."

Normally, salespeople try to tell their prospect why they don't want to just send over information, but they don't take the time to look at it from the prospect's point of view. This new process was a bait and switch, where I made these businesspeople feel like they were about to get the numbers. In truth, I had no intention of sending a proposal before our representative had paid them a visit, and with good reason.

I would reiterate my strong desire to send the prospect anything they wanted, but then I would reason with them so they could see the folly of getting a proposal before a presentation. I explained we didn't have any stock numbers or set prices as the costs depended largely on the specific needs of each company. I would get them to acknowledge this point by asking them, "Aren't you different from your competitor down the block?" Of course, every company wanted to see themselves as unique, so everyone answered in the positive that they were different.

Then I would tell them that even if I did give them some numbers over the phone, they would likely turn out to be too high or too low:

"If I gave you high numbers, then that might kill your interest right here and now, but if we have time to perform our analysis, it might produce lower numbers and vice versa. I could give you some low-ball numbers, and this would lead you down the road toward moving forward, but then, when we did the analysis, we could discover the real price is much higher. What you want is an accurate price so you can make a true comparison.

"However, I would love to save you some time because you may not want to do business with us no matter what our price is. I'm sure you only do business with companies you trust, correct? In that case, let me propose that we send our rep out briefly to explain the benefits, so you can make sure you even want to get the numbers. More importantly, this will give you a chance to judge our company to see if you want to do business with us. If you like us and want to get some comparative numbers, then the rep will have the information we need to produce an accurate proposal. Do you have your calendar open?"

(I will discuss the significance of these questions later in the book when we review closing strategies.)

Once I mastered this powerful reasoning tool, I finally started hitting the numbers I talked about at the beginning of this book. I still remember the first day I was able to post fifteen appointments with C-level decision makers on my company's sales board. I worked the time zones from East to West (as you do with a national company) and watched with excitement as my system allowed me to hit my appointment goal in just eight hours. I kept that pace for over six months!

Chapter 6

# ATTITUDE IS EVERYTHING, BUT WHAT KIND OF ATTITUDE?

The phrase "attitude is everything" is a common one in the business world. However, I have always felt the statement begs the question, "What kind of attitude?"

Years ago, I tried to quit smoking. After several failed attempts, I started to doubt if I truly believed I could successfully stop the habit. Even more, observing my own thought process caused me to wonder how it would ever be possible to know if a person who professes belief does truly believe.

When it comes to attitude, the truth isn't simply a matter of black and white. Just because someone doesn't seem to believe doesn't mean they completely lack faith. In reality, people can have degrees of faith. The way to know if someone truly believes something is when they take the necessary action.

If you find yourself in a situation like mine, where you feel you believe something strongly but are not taking action, then the truth is you will need to bolster what little belief you have, and build on that faith until you can finally manifest it as action.

I discovered this other piece to this puzzle quite by accident. One day, I showed up for work after having stayed out all night at a party. Though I was determined to reach my daily goal, I knew I wasn't going to turn in a stellar performance as I was completely exhausted. Even after drinking several sodas, I was still having a hard time keeping my eyes open.

My exhaustion caused me to have a kind of a flippant or cavalier attitude about my calling that day. However, despite this laid-back mood, I had enough persistence to at least keep dialing all day long, albeit with a less enthusiastic sales pitch than usual. Surprisingly, when the smoke cleared from that day, it turned out I had set five appointments, which easily bested the rest of the team.

How did I do so well?

Why didn't the fact that I hadn't had any sleep, wasn't all there, and exhibited an "I don't care" attitude have a negative effect on me? Strangely, it wasn't until I watched the movie X-Men: First Class that I was finally able to articulate exactly what had happened to me that day.

In X-Men: First Class, there is a scene where Professor X is training Magneto to harness his full power. Originally, Magneto had discovered quite tragically that rage was the key to unlocking a portion of his ability. However, with Professor X's help, he is able to see that blending emotions will allow him to harness his full strength. That's how later in the film Magneto is suddenly able to move an enormous structure, once he blends his rage with sadness. The movie showed me that when we blend two critical success traits, we can move mountains.

So what were the critical traits I exhibited that day? One of them was determination. Other than attitude, it is what is required to be a successful cold caller or salesperson.

However, there is a downside to this quality that must be taken into account. As salespeople, we must remain vigilant that determination does not become desperation, which is one of the world's greatest repellants. The second a businessperson detects even a trace amount of desperation in a salesperson, they will run for the hills. It's the same as when a single person becomes desperate to find a date and ends up scaring away everyone within a fifty-mile radius.

Desperation is poisonous to any marketing effort, and a salesperson who is absolutely determined to set an appointment can find that the longer this goal eludes her, the greater the danger of slipping into desperation. I know because this happened to me more times than I would care to admit.

One of the factors that can trigger desperation is your calling patterns. This happened to me once when it was taking a long time to get a closed appointment. I responded by dialing faster and pitching prospects I knew weren't qualified. Sometimes I would even skip my break. Needless to say, the faster I dialed, the more I hastened my transformation into a revolting Hyde reeking of desperation and scaring away all the prospects. This is why 100 percent determination can be extremely dangerous!

However, what if we could mix that determination with another quality that would balance it out? That day of successful calling, it wasn't just my persistence that brought me results. It was also my nonchalant style. When you pair the two, it gives birth to confidence.

Confidence is the polar opposite of desperation as it draws people to you instead of driving them away. Prospects want to speak with confident people, and as a result, it's "easy breezy" to persuade them to set up face-to-face meetings or give you their social security number. At MBNA America, my confidence made me the king of getting social security numbers. It was not uncommon for other agents to motion me over when they got stuck on a call because a prospect refused to relinquish their personal information. When I picked up the receiver and started projecting confidence, all the client's concerns would magically melt away!

To be a successful cold caller, you need an unflappable

determination combined with a nonchalant attitude, which when combined equals confidence. In short, we can rewrite the mantra to say that confidence is everything!

Chapter 7

# HOW TO QUICKLY GENERATE CONFIDENCE

I believe most people will readily agree that projecting confidence is important to gaining success. However, the common objection is: "It's great to be a confident person, but if you don't already possess confidence, how on earth can you harness it?"

The truth is we all have the power to change our minds quickly since our general attitude is merely a projection of what we are thinking in the moment. I'm not suggesting you can just tell yourself you are confident, and then you will magically transform into the very picture of self-reliance. However, it is almost that easy once you understand the principles behind what causes us to become nervous.

In my childhood and early teens, I was not a very self-assured person. When I faced a "fight or flight" scenario, my nerves would quake, causing me to receive more than my fair share of black eyes and bloody noses.

This problem followed me into young adulthood, where I faced an even greater challenge: public speaking. My early attempts at giving talks led to violent butterflies, cold sweats, mild quivers, and fast-talking. These symptoms lasted for some time until I learned that it was just a matter of chemistry. As you know, our body will often release adrenaline into our bloodstream when we confront our fears, and this was the chemical to blame for my nervous reaction to stressful situations.

You've probably heard stories of how people have performed uncanny feats when facing life-or-death situations. I heard one story of a man who was able to lift a three-thousand-pound car with his bare hands off a woman who was pinned down underneath the vehicle. These superhuman feats are possible when individuals have massive amounts of adrenaline released into their system, triggered by fear or panic.

If what I am describing sounds like your reaction to the idea of cold calling prospects, then take heart because those who are aware of the problem also have the remedy right in palm of their hands. While you may not always be able to transform your energy into "super powers," through a simple breathing and thought exercise, you can harness your natural ability to become confident—to turn your greatest weakness into your greatest strength.

The first step is to be cognizant when fear is triggering the release of adrenaline into your bloodstream and take action before the negative side effects have a chance to take over. This starts with calmly taking rhythmic deep breaths and giving yourself a pep talk. (Don't worry; you don't have to talk out loud.)

In private or within your mind, take yourself aside and speak to yourself like a coach giving a pep talk to one of his players. As you do so, take long deep breaths. The breathing will give power to your positive thoughts and slow the release of adrenaline so it can be controlled.

This is how I managed to overcome the fear of speaking in front of a group of people. While taking deep breaths, I would have a "silent" pep talk with myself to eliminate my fears. It wasn't as simple as saying, "Okay, I'm now confident." Instead, I would recite credible reasons for that confidence. I would remind myself that I was the one who developed the material in the speech I was about to deliver. This meant I must know the material since I was the one who dreamed it up in the first place.

I would also tell myself I wasn't going to go out there to merely avoid failure. Instead, I was going to boldly use hand gestures, make eye contact, pause for effect, use sense stress, and just pour my very soul into the speech. This breathing technique, combined with my powerful self-talk, produced an altered reality which slowed time and gave me a feeling of euphoria.

Several years ago, I had an opportunity to test this technique on someone else. My son was around ten years old and had just switched from playing chess to baseball, but unlike most of his teammates who had been indoctrinated in the sport from an early age, he didn't have a background playing baseball and was learning everything for the first time. Needless to say, he was behind the rest of the team.

We did what we could for him. We got him a coach on the side and began taking him to the indoor batting cages, but in spite of our best efforts, his performance continued to lag behind the rest of the team's during games. One day when we just happened to be rushing to one of his games, my son expressed his concern that our rushing meant he wouldn't have a chance to practice, and he pessimistically predicted he would turn out yet another dismal performance. That's when I decided it was time to teach him how to harness his adrenaline and tap into his subconscious mind.

I started by attacking his negative belief that lack of practice had sabotaged his chances of playing well in the game. I told him of a program I watched years ago showing an experiment researchers conducted with basketball teams to demonstrate the power of visualization. One team was allowed to practice free throws on the court each day during the experiment, while the other team was told not to practice on the court but instead spend the same amount of time visualizing shooting free throws in their mind.

When the week was up, they tested both teams to see which one would be able to hit more free throws. As it turned out, the team that visualized their shots outscored the team with the apparent advantage of physical practice!

I told my son he didn't necessarily need the practice before the game to ensure success. Instead, he could tap into something much more powerful: meditating on his practice. Reluctantly, he agreed to give it a try.

I told him to close his eyes and see the ball coming toward him and him perfectly executing the swing his coach had taught him. I asked him to think about this repeatedly and visualize seeing the ball connect with the bat. Then I told him to repeat to himself: "I'm going to hit the ball and make a play." I explained to him that the more he visualized it, the more power he would have to make it happen. I wanted him to see it until he believed he could hit that ball.

He followed through and kept up his mantra until he was in the batter's box. When the pitcher threw out his first pitch, my son connected with the ball like he had never done before in an actual game. The ball flew way out into the outfield and allowed him to get to third base! Of course, the cherry on top was when another player's hit allowed my son to come home and get his first point on the scoreboard.

This experience with my son left no doubt in my mind that we can have far more control of our abilities than most people realize. If picking up the telephone makes you feel like you're about to get up on a stage in front of a large crowd or evokes the fight-or-flight response, I recommend you unleash your inner powerhouse by utilizing your own breathing exercise and self-talk. Make sure you think about valid reasons why you should have confidence. Think about the training you have received, the books you have read, past experiences selling, etc.

While you're breathing, relive your past successes and remember your training, and you will feel the power begin to surge through you. You will transform yourself into a superhuman on natural steroids who has the ability to accomplish unbelievable results.

Chapter 8

# GETTING PAST THE GATEKEEPER

Of course, you can never increase your contacts or make more appointments if you can't even get out of the starting gate. For phone sales, this means bypassing the receptionist.

Most cold callers get stuck at the receptionist. It was a frustrating obstacle for me as well. My approach at first was to just try random techniques, hoping something would work. But I knew, if I would ever have a chance at setting fifteen appointments a day, I would eventually need to crack the enigma once and for all.

**Call From a Local Number**

After I began thinking about this problem, there were

several easy solutions that dawned on me right away, some which are still overlooked by most companies. The most obvious of these was the realization that the average, run-of-the-mill business prefers to do business with local companies. So that means when a receptionist sees a call coming in from a long-distance number, she's nine times more likely to screen it.

The simple solution is to ensure that salespeople always make outbound calls using a number that is local to the area they are calling. There are many ways to accomplish this if you're using a VOIP phone system, but if you don't know how or don't have access to such a system, make it your first priority to consult with a technology firm to find a workable solution.

**Enlist the Support of an Ally**

When a certain barrier prevents you from going directly to your destination and is so tall as to make climbing over it an impossibility, the only option left is to go around it. This is the exact technique I recommend you avail yourself of when the opportunity presents itself.

The first thing you must understand is receptionists don't exhibit the same defensive posture for every employee in the company. Normally, they will only raise their guard when you try to reach one of the executives. In other cases, they will direct you to the appropriate department.

If you attempt to get in touch with, for example, the accounting department, the gatekeepers will most likely assume you are calling to pay a bill. However, if you ask for the sales department, they won't be able to transfer the call fast enough because they will think you are a prospect. You can take advantage of these weaknesses by calling and trying to reach lower-level people in the company either by asking the receptionist or by using the phone directory. Once you've reached someone who probably doesn't get many solicitations, they will probably be more inclined to help you in your quest to reach the decision maker.

I can recommend two different strategies for leveraging your contacts. When the accountant or salesperson comes on the line, you can sound surprised and say you were trying to reach the decision maker, and that you must have either dialed or been transferred to the wrong extension. Then you can engage in a little small talk with this contact by asking what they do for the company, eventually coming around to asking them for help. Most of the time, these individuals won't mind helping, and you can ask if they will look up the contact's extension number to verify you have the correct one, or simply ask them to transfer the call directly to the decision maker.

I learned this strategy from other salespeople who got transferred to me and asked for me to transfer them to our president's extension. However, it wasn't until this happened to me a few times that it finally occurred to me what these savvy salespeople were actually doing: completely bypassing our gatekeeper!

If you always remember that you can go around the

receptionist and engage the help of a low-level employee, you will dramatically boost your contact ratio, which will ultimately help you reach your appointment setting goals.

**Use Vagueness and Double Meanings**

One of the most powerful tools a cold caller can use to bypass phone screeners is vagueness and phrases with potential double meanings. This comes into play when you greet the operator or receptionist and announce the purpose of your call.

One of the ways inexperienced agents often wrongly apply this principle is to outright lie and say they are returning the prospect's call. This can get you through the screening process and directly in touch with the decision maker, but these executives will spot your lie immediately when they realize they never called you and just hang up. Outright lying to the receptionist is not something we advocate in this book!

However, while outright lying is discouraged, there are key words and phrases that people can understand in multiple ways. One phrase is, "I'm calling back for John." At first glance, you might say that if John hasn't called you first, this is still a lie. But what if you have tried to reach John several times, and now you are trying to reach him again? You can truthfully say you are calling back for John.

If the receptionist understands this to mean their executive has called you and you're returning their call, that is not your fault. And when the ultimate contact asks you if they had called you, you can honestly say no, but you have tried to reach them several times before. As far as the decision maker is concerned, you have told the truth. It was just their receptionist who didn't clearly understand what you meant. Nine times out of ten, the contact will hear your full presentation.

Another vague statement comes in handy when answering the question, "What is this call about?" Over a long period of cold calling, it dawned on me I could say, "I'm calling regarding a financial matter." In most of these cases, I was usually trying to reach the CFO or controller within the company on my list, and just about any conversation I would have with them would be financial in nature. However, this phrase is vague enough to make it sound like I have an existing business relationship with the prospect.

**Go Around**

There is no need to run into a brick wall over and over again. Instead, stop and look to see if there is a way around. One technique I discovered to go around the receptionist was to take note of the companies on my list that utilized an automated phone system.

Make sure to note the companies that use an automated phone system so you can skip the operator/receptionist and get automatically transferred to the decision maker's phone. Often if you have the full name of your prospect, you can avoid pressing zero for the receptionist by selecting the dial by name option and simply spelling out their name. Then, when you get their voice mail, it will announce their extension, and this will allow you to record that number, so you can just dial their extension directly in the future.

### Shift Your Mindset

During my time getting past and around receptionists, it occurred to me that, while there are the dreaded gatekeepers out there that will try to stop your call no matter what, there are also many receptionists who are more easygoing.

I know what you're thinking: "If this is true, then how can so many calls get screened and ultimately blocked?"

The truth is most receptionists will put your call through, but it is the attitude and actions of the typical cold caller that are transforming the normal friendly receptionist into Mr. Hyde. The most detrimental attitude is the belief that most receptionists are hard-core phone screeners. This attitude often becomes a self-fulfilling prophecy and, more than anything, is what can trigger a negative phone-screening response from receptionists.

So, everybody, repeat after me: "Not every receptionist is a gatekeeper." Again, "Not every receptionist is a gatekeeper!" Once you truly believe that mantra, you will be ready to learn the true secrets of getting past the receptionist.

### Act Important

I learned this secret in my social life outside of work when a friend of mine told me how to stop paying cover charges at certain venues.

When he first told me this, I mocked him and reacted with utter disbelief. So to prove his point, he took me to a downtown bar that charged a cover and began to instruct me in the art of portraying absolute confidence. He told me I should act like I owned the place and just walk in while completely ignoring the people at the booth collecting the money. "Just walk right in and sit down," he said. He explained that this would create doubt on the part of the bouncers that perhaps I was someone important they shouldn't charge, and that if they harassed me, they might get into trouble. Well, I followed his instructions to a tee and was amazed to find myself sitting at the bar without paying a cover, and no one was harassing me!

That night a light bulb went off in my head as I realized that absolute confidence would be another key to getting past receptionists who were not true gatekeepers.

When you talk to a receptionist, you have to think of your call as critically important and act like you know the contact (without lying of course). The way to accomplish this is to simply state your first name, and then ask for your call to be transferred to the intended contact by using their first name. I can't underscore enough how important your attitude is in this situation. You need to project that you're somebody very important, so much that they feel like they might get into trouble if they questioned you.

Once you can make calls and project that kind of confidence, you will have the power to write your own check in paid commissions because nothing will be able to stop you! Combine that confidence with the next point in the process and you will be an absolute silver-tongued devil.

### Make Them Feel Important

I learned this other technique from Dale Carnegie's How to Win Friends and Influence People.

You see, all of us crave the feeling of importance, even more so than money in most cases. When you can make someone you're speaking with feel important, they will become putty in your hands. This applies to receptionists just as much as anyone.

So how do we make these phone screeners feel important? One of the strategies I use is to assume that, when I call the receptionist, the person answering the phone IS the decision maker. In other words, I assume the receptionist is important. I can tell you that this always makes the person I am speaking with feel good, and every once in a while, they actually turn out to be the real decision maker!

You can go ahead and think the people you meet or speak with are not important, but you are only going to shoot yourself in the foot. This scene happens in a lot of movies as it turns out the person they asked to get their coffee turns out to be the president of the company. Now repeat after me: "I will assume that everyone I speak with is important!"

### Use Sincere Compliments

The other way to make receptionists feel important is to compliment them, but I am not talking about mere flattery. You need to do better than some stock compliment you use on every call. This means you have to listen until you find something real. For example, when the person answering the business line gives you a perfect greeting, you can pause and ask if this is a live call or an answering machine and go on to explain that their greeting sounded so perfect, you thought it was rehearsed and recorded.

Another quality I listen for is the quality and professionalism of the phone greeter's voice. If their voice sounds professional, then I ask them if they were ever a DJ or an announcer. The key is to intently listen and try to discern something you can sincerely compliment.

When I compared the calls where I have complimented the receptionist with the times I didn't, I saw a dramatic increase in my rate of closing appointments. And if you combine sincere compliments with making your objective sound fun, then who in the world could ever say no to your request?

The key is to put the receptionist in a good mood. This will grease the machinery that normally locks you out of a transaction and transform a nearly impossible task into something rather easy. Think back to when you were a teenager. When was the best time to ask your parents for the keys to the family car? When they are in a good mood, right?! The same theory applies to getting a receptionist to transfer your call!

**Try to Blend In**

I learned something else when I started making business-to-business calls that will also help you get past the phone screener.

I started out in telemarketing by calling consumers, and there you normally had a fifty-fifty chance of connecting with your primary contact (i.e., the husband or wife) on the first call. When I transitioned to calling businesses, I was a little apprehensive since I figured that the companies we called would be busy conducting business, and our telemarketing calls would be intrusive. However, once I started in the new job, I realized the impressive array of phone traffic companies have to deal with on a daily basis.

A typical executive tasked with leading a company is responsible for researching the changing marketplace and staying ahead of the competition. With all the vendors trying to educate businesses on new trends, products and services, all these corporate officers really have to do is just sit back and decide which phone calls they want to take. And that responsibility is largely passed off to the receptionist. When you realize this, it should be apparent that the key to getting past phone screeners involves blending into the normal run-of-the-mill phone traffic receptionists have to deal with on a daily basis.

To master this, I thought back to when I worked at a company where we had to take random calls and tried to remember how those people who had business relationships with us would act when they called. As I remembered it, the calls were extremely informal. The representatives didn't announce the name of their company (a dead giveaway that you're calling to sell something), nor did they give out their full name. They also didn't ask for the full name of the contact. They simply said, "This is Bob calling for Jason…"

Of course, at this point, you should already have the contact's name. When you're cold calling to set appointments, you should never ask for the contact without knowing their name. If you're not aware of this point, then go back and read the section on qualifying your leads!

When you make a cold call without the exact name of your contact, then you have to try to extract that information from the receptionist. This will automatically alert them that you are probably a salesperson and trigger their metamorphosis into the dreaded gatekeeper. Making this blunder, more than anything else, can dramatically slow your contact ratio and keep you further away from reaching your goal of setting fifteen appointments a day.

**Use Mirroring**

The next lesson I learned that greatly aided me in connecting with receptionists and building rapport was the concept of mirroring. You can mirror both attitudes and voice patterns, including volume.

When an upbeat salesman calls in to a receptionist, often these individuals are not nearly as excited about their job as you probably are. This means they will often speak slower and with lower tones. Not only does sounding so chipper give you away as a salesperson and cause you to be screened, but it also rubs the receptionist the wrong way.

Just imagine approaching someone who has a major hangover, and you start speaking to them loudly and excitedly. The person with the hangover is going to immediately stop you and let you know you need to speak softer and slower or not at all. The same phenomenon happens when people are just waking up, have "not had their coffee," or are trying to recover from a heavy lunch. This is also true at the end of the day, when receptionists are ready to go home.

The key here is to identify their tone of voice and attitude, and then mirror that personality back. Be aware of the time of day you are calling, and anticipate the appropriate attitude to project. For example, when I am calling into a time zone that's early in the morning, I always speak softly and slowly and even sometimes complain about not being fully awake because I "haven't had my coffee yet."

Another safe strategy is to project the dreary work life attitude. Many receptionists are not happy with their jobs. When I pick up on a negative vibe, I use phrases like: "You know, another day another dollar," or "They are making me work for a living." Most of the time the receptionist laughs at my folksy pessimism and offers her own negative cliché about work life.

The magic of imitating the attitudes of the receptionist is that people in general "like" other people that are like themselves. This applies to people who are from where you're from, dress like you dress or watch the movies you like, but it also applies to people who share your general sentiment and attitude about life. When you speak like the receptionist, they will most often feel an instant bond or connection with you and be far more inclined to listen to a modest request to have your call transferred. In essence, this is a quick shortcut for creating instant rapport!

**Never Ask if Your Prospect Is Available**

This next tip came to me as a result of actually listening to what receptionists told me when I asked them if my contacts were available. You see, time and again, they would place my call on hold and later return to either inform me the person was not in the office or start asking me for more information. Often, they would tell me the contact had requested that I just send information.

I repeated this boneheaded process for years until I truly reflected on it and realized I had just been setting myself up for failure all that time. I realized the receptionist was merely following my instructions to ascertain if the contact was IN the office or AT their desk.

What this meant was that they either buzzed their line or physically went to the contact's office to see if they were at their desk. When the receptionist found the person I was trying to reach, they probably informed them there was a call waiting for them. This inevitably triggered a chain reaction, where the primary contact inquired as to who exactly was calling for them and what they wanted. This caused the receptionist to become a liaison, now screening my call at the request of the primary contact.

Do you see how I set myself up for failure?

There is a much better way to approach this, and that is by never asking the receptionist if your prospect is available, at their desk, or in the office.

Instead, just ask is if the receptionist can "try their line," and tell them that if the contact isn't there, you will simply leave a voice message. This will save the receptionist time, so they won't have to go back and forth with the primary contact, completely bypassing the boneheaded "checking" process.

**Effective Voicemail Strategy**

Many of the business people I talk with are under the illusion that, if they can just leave a great voicemail, they can just sit back and wait for their prospects to call them back. I can tell you I have experimented with nearly every type of voicemail message there is, and the best you can ever hope for is to get one or two return calls, and typically, these people didn't understand the message or are just not good prospects.

The danger with leaving detailed voicemails about who you are and why you are calling is that you end up just educating the contact enough to avoid your call. This sabotages the entire cold-calling strategy of making contact through curiosity.

Curiosity is when the primary contact takes your call because they are not sure who is calling and whether it's important or not. If you leave a detailed voicemail, then more often than not, when you call back, they will be able to connect your name to the message you left, and this will remove all doubt that you're a salesperson. Also, with detailed messages, you run the risk of leaving a record of the number of times you called. This can cause a prospect to feel that you're phone stalking them, and when this happens, I promise you will never reach that decision maker in a million years!

So while you're actively trying to make immediate contact with these prospects, avoid leaving any voicemails, and only leave voicemails with contacts you are unable to reach over a period of a few weeks. Then you can compile a list of these hard-to-reach contacts, and when appropriate, leave all your messages at once.

The most effective voicemails are those that are extremely vague. This leads a potential client into thinking you might be an important prospect for them. A vague voicemail omits the name of the company you're calling from and even the purpose of your call. Instead, say only your name and that you're trying to reach them.

Of course, after you have left a few of these vague voicemail messages with these hard-to-reach prospects, you can advance to leaving a more detailed message later. Just remember that, in most cases, these messages will be heard several days or weeks later. Therefore, it's important you leave a high-quality message that resembles a radio spot, where you get your unique selling proposition across in a dramatic fashion!

If you follow this process, then you will get more return

calls, and they will likely turn out to be good prospects who both understand what you are offering and have an interest in setting an appointment to meet with a salesman. Cha-ching!

**How to Deal with Real Gatekeepers**

As I've intimated earlier, encounters with real gatekeepers are just about as rare as seeing a shark on a snorkel excursion. But these overzealous phone screeners do in fact exist, and when you make contact with one, there is almost nothing you can do to avoid the direct questions they will ask to discover if you're making a sales call. Once you're exposed, they will always direct your call to the obligatory voicemail system where failed cold calls go to die.

But take heart. There is a counterintuitive approach that can get you through this obstacle, at least some of the time. The key is to understand that these difficult phone screeners feel important and proud of their ability to catch salespeople trying to reach their decision makers. You need to acknowledge that.

The secret to achieving at least some marginal success when facing this rare foe is to first identify that you're actually speaking with one of the true gatekeepers, and then be absolutely honest with them about who you are, the company you're calling from, and the purpose of your call. The last thing you want to be is vague with these formidable opponents.

Remember, everybody wants to feel important! And as Dale Carnegie says, if you know how someone gets their feeling of importance, you know exactly how to deal with them.

I use this principle when I have to deal with a police officer who has stopped me for speeding. The first thing I do is get out all my paperwork, including my license and my insurance. Then when the policeman approaches my vehicle, I give that to the officer and openly admit I was speeding and deserve a ticket. This works most of the time for two basic reasons.

First, these actions are the exact opposite of what the officer expects, and second, I have taken away the officer's chance to get his feeling of importance from lecturing me after I have given an excuse or denied speeding. I have forced the officer into a position where the only way he can get the same feeling of power and importance is by just issuing a warning and letting me off the hook. When you deny or make excuses, it just encourages the officer to feel powerful by slapping you with an expensive speeding ticket!

You are doing the same thing with the gatekeepers who get their power from catching salespeople trying to trick their way through the screening process. When you openly admit what you're doing, then these gatekeepers will have to get their power of importance by switching from blocking you to allowing you to get through to the decision maker. Amazing, right?

## Counterintuitive Holding Strategy

When telephone prospecting, it's common to encounter gatekeepers who say the decision maker is on another call and then ask if you want to hold. The normal gut reaction of any marketing agent is to decline and move on to the next call. Before you hang up the phone, though, stop and consider if doing the opposite might actually increase your contact ratio?

The common wisdom regarding holding for a cold call is that it's a waste of time since you will most likely wait for a long time and still end up not speaking with the decision maker. Traditional thinking assumes the span of time wasted on holding could be used to dial more numbers and possibly make another contact. I used to subscribe to this same logic.

However, after examining the evidence and practicing some trial and error, I came around to a bit of counterintuitive reasoning. I began to question the logic of refusing to hold for decision makers and began to believe that doing the opposite might be the key to increasing my contacts.

Usually, if you make one solitary call to a list of prospects, you will likely hear the same response after every failed attempt: "You've just missed them." So if, instead, you hear, "They are on another call," that is an opportunity. The vast majority of calling agents will assume gatekeepers are only saying the decision makers are on another call as a ploy to block their efforts to make contact, but these executives really are taking one conference call after another and moving in and out of conference rooms all day long. Remember, receptionists are acting as a sort of air traffic controller and are generally not all out to block you. So when they say the person you're trying to reach is "on the phone," they're probably telling the truth.

When you decide to hold for these prospects, you will be following the sage advice of Aesop: "A bird in hand is worth two in the bush." The bird in hand is the executive you're on hold with, who will most likely speak with you if you will patiently wait for them. However, when you refuse to hold and continue prospecting, then you are in effect chasing after all the elusive prospects "in the bush."

The reason this technique is so powerful is because it's the exact opposite of what most telemarketing agents would ever do. As soon as you communicate to the receptionist you are in fact willing to hold, you have just convinced them this can't possibly be a solicitation. Salespeople never hold!

At the same time, this action conveys that your call is important since you're actually willing to hold. And when you spend several minutes holding for a decision maker, it will make them feel important knowing you are willing to wait to speak with them. Using this technique will dispel any doubt on behalf of the executive that you're making a sales call. This in turn will dramatically increase the possibility of getting through to that all-important contact.

Using this holding strategy can only translate into a massive increase in your contact ratios. Just a word of caution, though: it's important that you don't wait too long for one contact and that you don't expect this strategy to work every time you decide to hold. However, I have found that the percentage of success is way over 60 percent, which means the positives of holding far outweigh the negatives.

When I was writing this section of the book, I was also working on a marketing campaign setting appointments in Houston for a cloud provider. I had just set up fifteen meetings for the prior week. However, my contacts were very low, and this prevented me from setting up a lot more sales meetings. So I turned to the holding strategy and was able to double my contacts. When I started telling receptionists that I was willing to hold for the prospect, I was able to squeeze another ten appointments from the same size list!

I should warn you that some receptionists get very uneasy having people on hold, so it is not uncommon for them to constantly check in and make sure you "still" want to hold for the executive. When this happens, do what you can to set them at ease. I love to help them relax by saying I was killing time checking my stocks or that I love the hold music. Mainly, I reassure them they don't need to keep checking in on me as I am willing to wait for the long haul.

If you handle this right, the receptionist will let you remain on hold; but if you sound like you're unhappy holding, then they will often pressure you to either leave a message or call back. Don't take this bait! Remember that if you are on hold, you really have a solid opportunity! So be polite and be patient, and holding will convince both the phone screener and the decision maker that you're not a salesperson.

**Last-Ditch Effort**

When all else fails, you can always resort to making up a completely ridiculous line that will make the executive contact you're trying to reach laugh. Typically, I only use this when I am having an extremely bad day reaching decision makers or on a lead that is about to go into my voicemail filter.

When I reach this point, I will say I am a snake oil salesman selling only the best snake oil for businesses. When all else fails, I can attest that this humorous approach can work to get both the phone screener and the contact's attention! So give it a try. If you don't want to use my snake oil line, be creative and come up with your own ridiculous idea. But use it sparingly. This is a last resort.

Chapter 9

# DIVISION OF LABOR: QUALIFYING YOUR LIST

Looking at the business world today, Adam Smith, the father of modern economics, must be rolling over in his grave. This is the visionary who saw how both specialization and division of labor could benefit production. However, if you fast-forward hundreds of years, you can see that, unless a company is involved in manufacturing, they have completely abandoned these concepts.

When I started working at CSI as an appointment setter, it quickly became apparent to me that I was working within a broken system. When our CRM manager loaded in new leads, this would drastically slow our contact ratios due to a glaring lack of information. This meant we had to spend our time calling to learn about the company structure and who the decision maker was. Often, without knowing the number of employees a company had, I would waste days trying to reach a prospect and ultimately reach them, pitch them, and even close them, only to discover at the end of the call that they didn't have enough employees to qualify as a legitimate appointment.

What a waste of time!

When you think about the callers on your team, you will usually have some top representatives who are far better closers than the rest. Do you really want these hard-core cold callers wasting their time doing information gathering to scrub your call list?

No matter what industry you're representing when you make your cold calls, you're going to have some parameters that need to be verified. At the very least, not knowing the full name of the specific contact is going to be a red flag for phone greeters. Wouldn't your company gain efficiency if you dedicated some of your team to qualifying while the rest of your calling agents spent their precious time trying to reach decision makers to close deals or set appointments?

When I finally started my own telemarketing company, I can tell you the first thing I did was divide the labor and hire specific representatives to work as qualifiers. I found that three cross-trained agents could keep a team of four or five serious business cold callers supplied with enough qualified leads to be successful. When there was downtime, I transitioned these agents to working on our external marketing, such as Internet marketing, creating lists and qualifying appointments. All of this helped us keep a steady stream of clients flowing into the business, so that I always had enough work to keep the team busy.

If you happen to be a salesperson tasked to generate your own appointments, then no doubt you have experienced being stuck in the weeds qualifying your own telemarketing list. So what can you do?

First, you can outsource the qualifying process. This way the qualifying can get done while you're following up on leads and making sales presentations. Outsourcing is something that companies can also look at if they don't have a large enough telemarketing team to divide the labor. The process of qualifying your telemarketing list is not extremely complicated, but it is very laborious and it's the type of repetitive work that is not normally appealing to salespeople or hard-core closers.

If outsourcing isn't possible and you have to handle qualifying yourself, first check the "About Us" or "Contact Us" section of your prospect's website. Any of those web pages can contain an employee list where you can glean the title, e-mail, and either a direct dial number or an extension. All of this information is extremely valuable when getting past gatekeepers.

Hopefully the CRM you have chosen to use in your cold-calling endeavors will be robust enough to have a field for websites, and the list you purchase will come with enough data for qualifiers merely to click the website link on the contacts page of the CRM. One of the list providers I have used has the right data and that's ZoomInfo. The CRM or contact management system I use now is Salesforce. If you have these agents manually looking up the websites on Google, then you're going to waste a lot of precious time that could be spent actually gathering information. Also, if the list you're buying doesn't come with the website data and URL, then stop purchasing from that vendor.

In some cases the information listed on the website will be out of date, so it's always prudent to call the company to verify the information with the operator or receptionist. As you begin calling these companies directly and start asking the receptionist a lot of questions, often you will find they will raise their guard, especially when you try to discover the full name of their executives. When you encounter this situation, just gather what information the phone greeter is willing to divulge, and then get the receptionist to transfer you to that contact's voicemail. Very often, the name will either be announced by the voicemail system, or the contact will announce their full name in their voicemail greeting.

When you are qualifying and attempting to garner the name of executives, the one place you want to be sent is the voicemail. Of course, this only works if you employ a bit of reverse psychology, much like the rabbit begging the bear and fox not to throw him into the briar patch. If the receptionist won't reveal the name of the contact, go ahead and act disappointed. Then act like voicemail is the last place you want to go. This will keep the savvy receptionist from figuring out what you are up to.

You will find that most receptionists will be happy to divulge information if you approach them in the right manner. Essentially, the way to accomplish this is by telling them you're merely gathering information, so you can send the prospect some information before you try to contact them in person.

The most obvious place to start is by verifying the address of the company as this is the least threatening piece of information you could possibly ask for. It allows you to start small and then build by asking for more information. When it comes to getting the executive's name, the ideal way is to ask for the exact spelling of their name so you can address your information packet correctly. This will make it sound like you already know the name of the contact. As a whole, this process will net you all the information you need without raising the defenses of the receptionist or the operator.

The last piece of information you'll want to get is the e-mail address. I find that when you have successfully gotten the phone screener to verify and divulge the contact name, an easy way to get the email address is to simply ask, "Oh yeah, what's a good e-mail address for Bob?" You see once again, it sounds like you already have an e-mail address for your prospect but just need to make sure it's still correct.

You will often hear them start looking for the executive's email address and then start calling it out to you over the phone. Make sure you're ready to record this information in your CRM as you don't want to irritate them by asking for the data over and over again. However, it is appropriate to read the e-mail you record back to the receptionist to make sure you heard it correctly.

Once you have the full contact name of the prospect, the next place you should search for more information is the social networking sites like LinkedIn and Facebook. Here, these executives might have more valuable information that can be harvested to aid salespeople with the rapport-building process. Agents should look for the decision makers' school affiliations, groups they belong to, especially where they may volunteer, and their interests such as golf, reading, travel, etc. Again, this is information your qualifiers can gather if your organization has properly divided the labor.

Chapter 10

# WHO IS YOUR TARGET AUDIENCE?

So which type of prospect should you be targeting? This is a subject of vital importance because the conventional sales and marketing wisdom dictates that prospecting efforts should be targeting prospects who have "needs" and "pain points."

Don't get me wrong. Finding prospects who are extremely unhappy with their current service and highly motivated to change is awesome, but I have found that the odds of stumbling upon a company whose executives are willing to communicate their pain and frustration about their current vendors is extremely rare. The vast majority of prospects will normally communicate they are happy with their current vendor.

Of course, the reality is that many of these people do actually have some issues in the back of their minds, but these factors haven't caused them to reach their "boiling point." The only way to secure an appointment with these poker-faced decision makers is to agree with them, talk about their future needs and ultimately get them to agree that, when it comes to their decisions for the future, they are willing to keep an open mind.

This strategy works because it has been working for me for over fifteen years. The absolute last thing you ever want to do when speaking with a prospect who professes to be happy is try to use the "Sandler Approach" of probing for pain points. According to Ganesha Khalsa, founder and CEO of the Sandler Training Institute, the key objective of a Sandler-trained sales rep is to "first convince the buyer that he or she has specific technical needs."

This is a caveman tactic that will only cause your prospect to put up walls. They won't want to reveal any negative information because such self-disclosure in their mind will only diminish their negotiating power or make them look bad. To understand this, we need to go behind the walls of a business and look into the minds of executives to see what motivates them to change.

We can all agree that most vendor relationships are fairly tough to break. Most companies hate the idea of change, like their vendors, and don't have time to make comparisons.

Unless business operations have come to a grinding halt as a result of a vendor's failure, they normally won't entertain shopping around.

But even if things aren't quite right with a vendor, executives are usually not willing to communicate their latent needs to an outsider. Why? This is a legitimate question that I believe could best be answered with a bit of self-examination. You wouldn't go around telling strangers or even friends about embarrassing problems you caused because of poor decision-making, would you? Of course not! None of us really ever wants to admit when we have made a mistake, and we will usually go to great lengths to hide such facts.

So why would we believe that executives would want to reveal their mistakes any more than you or I would? Especially when those mistakes seem manageable for the time being. The truth is that even one episode of a vendor disaster isn't normally enough to tip the scales of pain and need in an executive's mind. It's not uncommon for executives to give vendors turning in subpar performances plenty of time to improve. Better that than having to admit they made a mistake picking the vendor in the first place.

When a manager or owner does finally reach their boiling point, it usually means they have run out of options and face dire consequences. This pressure can cause even the shrewdest negotiator to lose their cool and forget their poker face.

These facts on the surface seem to validate the view most

marketing professionals have of only targeting the companies that have already reached that boiling point. However, this narrow-minded view ignores the fact that there has to be a history of issues building up over time that may not have reached the total disaster level, but could still be inconvenient enough at some point to trigger an eruption of anger. These inconvenient incidences are what I call "latent needs:" issues that lurk just beneath the surface of a decision maker's mind.

If the business people who have latent needs and those who are in fact content with their vendors both say they are happy, then how can you tell them apart? The truth is that people don't always say what they mean, but their actions will speak louder than their words. This means that, when you speak with executives who say they are happy with their current vendor, you need to look for two possible outcomes. Either they maintain their position throughout the presentation and do not set an appointment, or they maintain their position and actually set up a meeting.

It's pretty clear that, when a prospect is adamant they don't want to change and maintain this posture throughout the conversation, they are telling the truth. However, if you can entice a prospect still claiming to be happy to set up a face-to-face meeting, then you have discovered a bona fide prospect with latent needs!

I discovered this when conducting a telemarketing campaign in Arkansas for a managed services provider. I made contact with a controller that was very nice but repeated several times during our conversation that she was happy with her current IT vendor. However, I used the techniques outlined in this book and was successfully able to persuade her to set an appointment to learn about a new improvement in the IT services industry—one that would allow companies to have a stable IT bill month-in, month-out, even when they have spikes in labor.

Even though the controller made it clear to me she was still happy with her current vendor and not looking to change, she still agreed to set up the meeting. Now, fast-forward to the point where this prospect had actually gone through the IT provider's full sales cycle and even received a proposal. When I followed up to see if she had any interest in moving forward with our proposal, she told me, "We solved that billing issue."

That was the end of the call, but did you catch that?

The whole time I was talking with that manager about our flat-fee billing structure, she was thinking in the back of her mind about the billing issues they were having with their current IT vendor. It was this billing issue that motivated her to set up that appointment and eventually get a proposal. However, she never communicated with me or the sales rep any information about this billing issue throughout the sales process. This exchange was the beginning of my understanding of how prospects can say they are happy when they really have issues.

Some skeptical readers might say that it was possible to

thing we need to do now is to decide on a start day."

I told her I would have Tony follow up with her, and when I heard that her law firm had closed, I literally got goose bumps. It was clear evidence that these types of prospects could be closed!

I got more confirmation of this when I spent a year-long sabbatical working for Commercial IT Solutions, another managed services provider, as a marketing director. During that time period, I was able to close fifteen to twenty cloud-computing contracts with lawyers, CPAs, associations, wealth management companies, and more. Every single one of these prospects was generated using the telemarketing system advocated in this book. In addition, all of the executives from these companies expressed at the outset that they were completely happy with their current IT provider but still ultimately signed cloud agreements with our company!

For me, this established once and for all that you can target companies that claim to be happy and still successfully close. In my next book, How to Turn the Golden Rule into Marketing Gold, I will discuss the sales I made during this time period and the process I used to effectively develop a relationship with all those companies. For our purposes, though, it should be enough to know from the examples I have cited that decision makers often say they are happy with their current services, but many times, this is not the absolute truth. Once you understand this, you should realize that it's entirely feasible to persuade these "happy" executives to book appointments.

You most definitely can sell to prospects that don't admit to having an immediate need! The techniques laid out in this book will help you successfully navigate the path to setting appointments with these types of leads. If you actually apply these principles, you will be able to generate more sales leads than you ever would dream possible!

Chapter 11

# THE PRESENTATION

I am a chess player at heart, and chess games are comprised of three main parts: the opening, the middle game, and the end game. This is how I suggest you tackle the most ambitious aspect of the sales cycle: the presentation.

The opening is exactly what it sounds like. It is the beginning of the presentation, where you explain to the prospect who you are and what you're calling about. In addition, you will make sure to get the prospect's attention and verify that you're both on the same page regarding the material you're presenting.

The middle game is where you actually deliver the meat of

your presentation and also discover more about the services the prospect currently has in place.

The end game naturally consists of overcoming objections and closing.

### The Opening

When you have reached your first goal of making contact with the decision maker, you should begin by saying a brief greeting and then verify who you are speaking with, along with their role within the company. The last thing you want to do is spill your guts to the wrong prospect, who is not even in a position to buy anything, much less set an appointment to meet with a representative.

Once you have checked that box, it's time to drop all the vagueness and double meanings and honestly tell the contact your name, the name of the company you're calling from, and finally your proposition. Don't forget to break the ice by trying to sincerely compliment the prospect on something you have observed about the company like their great website, amazing receptionist, positive attitude, great voice, or if you have researched their LinkedIn page, one of their interests or past accomplishments.

Breaking the ice by complimenting the executive is probably the most important steps in the presentation if you are ultimately going to close. It's important to take some time to develop your unique selling proposition (USP) as you really want it to communicate the type of business you're in, along with the major benefit of your product or service.

Take a page from those Machiavellian representatives who name congressional bills and craft a USP that sounds irresistible to your prospect—something like, "We're the company that helps you get more out of retirement plans," or "We help businesses avoid the red tape." Just keep it simple, and make sure it sounds tantalizing.

Remember that the primary goal of these steps is to ensure that the prospect knows exactly what you are going to be talking about. One of the greatest hazards that can develop is when agents fail to clarify in the mind of the prospect exactly what they're talking about. Eventually in the conversation, it will become apparent that the prospect is thinking about something completely different than what you were discussing, and this will come to haunt you at the end of the call when it's nearly too late to resolve.

Now let me splash some cold water on any excitement you may have about developing a unique selling proposition. Telling the prospect your primary benefit doesn't mean that you're gearing up to automatically knock that pitch out of the ballpark. I can assure you that, no matter how crafty your unique selling proposition sounds, most of the companies you're calling will say they are happy with all their current business services and are "all set."

We will be discussing how to overcome objections later in this section, but for now, it's important to know that by far the easiest way to overcome objections is to anticipate them and rebut them before the prospect actually raises the issue.

## The Million-Dollar Rebuttal

Since we know that the vast majority of prospects in the business world already strongly believe they have the best products and services in place, then right after you state your unique selling proposition, it's critical that you emphatically announce to the prospect you already know they have a service or product in place they're probably extremely happy with. Most likely this statement will take the contact totally by surprise, but even more importantly, it's a sentiment that executives are easily able to agree with.

As long as you advance propositions they are inclined to agree with, you will be able to keep the conversation going long enough to eventually close. If you follow this tactic, you will get over the first major barrier that blocks average cold callers from advancing to the middle game of the presentation.

Now that you have gotten the prospect to lower their guard by saying something that's universally agreeable, it's time to flip the script by saying something which negates the previous thought. I have found that most leaders will agree with the sentiment that everything is constantly changing.

The level of service they have with their current vendor may change, technology will change, the market could become more competitive, and prices could go down. In other words, it's always possible that there could be something out there that's better! The secret to getting past the barrier of "we're all set" hinges on getting the decision makers to agree that things are always changing and that it's possible there could be a better product or service out there.

Finally, you can transition them into the middle game by getting the prospect to confirm they do indeed keep their options open. Make absolutely sure, though, you wait long enough for the prospect to say something that signifies agreement, even if it's just a grunt. If you move forward in the conversation without getting the prospect to agree at each step, it's like building a house on sand, and you will see all your hard work collapse.

### Talking Out of Both Sides of Your Mouth

Let's be clear, when I am speaking about talking out of both sides of your mouth, I am not talking about lying. Instead, I am talking about a savvy individual who will intuit that humans are often of two minds, both tangible and intangible. This technique can also be called the pressure-and-release tactic.

You see, it's rather common for people, especially business leaders, to hold two directly conflicting thoughts or beliefs. While a prospect can be happy with their current services, it's possible for them to also be curious about what else might be available in the current market.

In addition, business consumers are plagued with an overwhelming fear of commitment and sales pressure. So you will have to conduct a balancing act while you move your presentation forward and advance your proposition. You will need to delicately go back at each step to remind the prospect that you're still aware that they are currently happy and not looking to change.

The reason I label this technique talking out of both sides of your mouth is because you are first making a statement that you understand that the prospect is happy, then you are making a contradictory statement that things are always changing and that it could be possible to find something better. You have to go back and forth with this tedious balancing act in order to keep both sides of the prospect's mind happy. This is how you tie up the fear side of the prospect's mind so it can't interrupt the sales process.

**The Middle Game**

The middle game is where you lay your foundation of interest by elaborating upon your unique selling proposition. In other words, you attempt to paint an alluring, detailed word picture that will build in the prospect a sense of intense curiosity.

You will know that you have safely landed in the middle game when you ask them the leading question that is meant to hook their interest and they allow you to proceed and make your presentation. This is where your research will pay off as you have looked at all the features of your product and have discovered the one that's most innovative, least known, or least understood. If you happen to be an owner or executive of a business going through this process, there are times where you will literally have to create this new added advantage.

Many times this will mean embracing a major shift in your marketplace, as Jim Collins describes in his book, Good to Great, once you have found this key new feature that's not well known in the marketplace, then you can lead off with your middle game question by asking, "Have you heard of _____?"

A very good example of what I am talking about, when describing this new element in your industry, would be the current shift in the IT support industry, moving from managing on premise IT networks to a total cloud-based network infrastructure known as desktop-as-a-service. This is a good example of a paradigm shift taking place in the IT industry that many good companies are completely ignoring to their peril.

In the print-and-copy space, the shiny new cool technology shift is called managing print. So we could use these market shifts as examples to frame our middle game question as follows: "Have you heard of desktop-as-a-service?" or "Have you heard of the managed print concept?" Both of these service delivery models represent something that most business executives are not fully educated about.

When I worked for a security distributor named Triad in Dallas, I became a phone salesman who had to keep calling on security companies to sell them an array of security products along with batteries and wire. However, I looked in every nook and cranny of their warehouse until I uncovered an array of cool technology that was literally collecting dust. One of the awesome paradigm shift concepts I uncovered was video alarm verification. While this would require new expensive alarm-monitoring equipment, it would also open the market for video cameras in homes.

I lead my marketing efforts by teaching the security companies in my territory about the new technology against the best efforts of the vice president of the company, who demanded I just sell batteries and wire. However, four months later, the sales reports showed that I had doubled the sales in my territories, all which sat outside of Texas and required expensive shipping costs. Guess what these companies were ordering from me? Batteries, wire, alarm panels, etc. Oh yeah, we also sold a couple of these twenty-to-thirty-thousand-dollar video alarm verification systems, much to the chagrin of the manager.

I mentioned this story to emphasize how important it is to have an innovative message leader in your marketing team. This will help your sales reps when they get their prospects to the middle game. Here is another example:

During the time I ran my call center, they paid me extra to travel and provide some additional sales training and coaching. However, the information I gathered from an IT client indicated their service model didn't have an innovative "bells and whistles" we could educate business owners about.

While I waited for the president of this ten-million-dollar IT company to meet with me, I spent my time trying to figure a way to communicate the importance of enhancing his service model. Unfortunately, the president was very close-minded, didn't listen to anything I had to say, and spent our time together trying to prove to me his current model worked just fine.

After our discussion, we left their posh offices to run the appointments my cold-calling team had set up for their company. At the last appointment, we met with the managing partner of a very successful law firm located in one of the tallest buildings in Dallas. The president took the lead in making the sales presentation to the lawyer, which centered on trying to find pain points. However, this lawyer just went on and on about how happy he was with his current IT provider.

Once the president grew tired of looking for pain points to capitalize upon, he looked at me in frustration and said, "Why are we here?" I decided to ignore his rude statement and take over the presentation, so I could show him how to sell when you have innovative services. Unbeknownst to the president, I had paid rapt attention to the attorney while he spun his yarn about how great his current tech company was in dealing with server crashes. As far as the president was concerned, the recovery time the lawyer was reporting was the same that his company would have been able to offer.

However, I was aware of new technology that neither the president nor the lawyer were aware of. Therefore, I started by asking the lawyer if he had heard of the innovative technology that would allow him to restore his crashed server faster! (This is the innovative disaster recovery solution that Datto currently offers.) After I finished explaining how this new disaster recovery technology worked, the lawyer changed his posture from trying to convince us he was all set to one of intense curiosity. He started asking me questions about how this system might work in his environment and even queried us about the price.

Of course, I was there representing a company that didn't even have the technology I was discussing, but I brought it up in an attempt to teach this arrogant president how important it is to conduct market research and make sure your service model always reflects state-of-the-art technology. As we left the appointment and headed back to our cars, this once close-minded president was actually asking me to tell him all about this new disaster-recovery system that had piqued the interest of the prospect.

Funny how showing always gets a better response than telling!

Most of the time, development of a business model is not viewed through the marketing lens; however, the reality is that each point in your product or service offering should be evaluated from a standpoint of how this will help you ultimately make more sales.

Hopefully you can learn from these examples that just marketing the nuts and bolts of your product or service does not give the sales team any sizzle on its own. You have to create curiosity. When you ask a prospect about new innovative services, an open-minded prospect will be forced to answer that they are not familiar with those concepts, and this opens the door to you offering them a path to innovation.

Of course, you may encounter prospects that will indicate

they have heard of your concept. This is when you can go a little bit deeper by asking penetrating follow-up questions: "Have you ever had a presentation on that?" "Have you ever looked at a proposal?" Nine times out of ten, you will get a "no." In this case, the "no" is exactly what you're looking for because the prospect has just given verbal permission to move forward with the middle game presentation.

Another common mistake that inexperienced cold callers make is to get nervous and essentially deliver a monologue instead of a presentation. When you do all the talking and don't ask questions that allow the prospect to speak, you're headed for disaster. Yes, you still might make it to the end of your pitch, but I can assure you, the typical prospect will have just been rehearsing the way they will tell you no the entire time you're speaking.

It is imperative you make the presentation a conversation, and the best way to do this is by asking specific questions that will allow you to remain in control of the discussion. Also, it's important to pause and listen when the prospect either answers your questions, makes a statement, or asks their own questions.

One of the best ways to ensure you're listening to the prospect when they speak is by writing down what they say. Having written notes on the conversation will also help you remember what they said when it's time to make your notes and disposition the call in the CRM.

Now it's time to get the conversation going the other

direction by asking the prospect to tell you about the product or service they have in place. You can even inquire as to the name of the current vendor if they don't mind disclosing that information. Then you want to ask about the level of services they are receiving, what comes with the current offer, and what costs them extra. There is also no harm in trying to discover what they are currently paying for their services. This is what I call probing the prospect as you look for weaknesses without pointing them out to the prospect.

After discovering an area where the decision makers have revealed they have an outdated or insufficient level of service, you must bite your tongue to ensure you never say anything negative about their current product or service. However, you most definitely should mark that down and later discuss how one of the benefits you are offering fills that gap.

A really good example of how to utilize this probing technique when selling IT services would be to ask about the type of disaster recovery your contact currently has in place. If this query is done in a nonthreatening way and follows your adamant insistence that you know the prospect is happy with their current vendor, then you should reasonably expect them to open up to discussing exactly what type of service they have in place.

For example, if you are offering a new cloud-based backup and find a lead is still using an older technology, like tape or disc, then you should make this one of the points you elaborate on during the middle game presentation. However, if you discovered the prospect has already updated their disaster recovery to the latest technology, then you should just keep probing for another weakness. I should warn newbie cold callers that omitting the probing technique will destroy the prospect's belief that you're truly interested in them or will be able to make knowledgeable suggestions. So asking these questions will help you in more ways than one.

I can relate from personal experience that I once had what I thought was a successful conversation that led all the way to the end game, only to be shocked to hear from the prospect that, since I never asked him any questions, they weren't interested, and there was no way he wanted to have a sales representative visit them. Please let my experience serve as a stark warning that motivates you to incorporate probing into your middle game presentation. Include this technique on a checklist that allows you to review your calls and verify you are truly implementing this style in your sales pitches.

All that remains in the middle game is to begin your pitch by highlighting that what you're about to describe represents a paradigm shift in the market. Before you start talking about how phenomenal your service is, though, it's important to stop and compliment them for having a well-thought-out plan in place.

For example, after the disaster recovery probe, you could state that computer disasters are a very serious problem that a lot of companies realize but fail to ever implement a strategy to correct. However, you are impressed that they have a good solution in place that's still working for them.

Now you can dive into extolling the top features and benefits of your amazing service. First, if you have a great illustration or example that does a really good job of getting your major point across, then this is a good place to toss that into the mix. When I was selling the employee leasing or PEO concept, our team would usually lead off with the following: "Wouldn't you agree that your employees are half an asset and half a liability?" Then we would explain that what employee leasing does is take control of the liabilities and leave the asset for them to control and manage.

Also, if there are some negative issues that continue to dog your company or industry, then the best policy is to just take the bull by the horns and bring those up before the prospect has a chance to raise the objection. This follows the example of legal defendants who have potentially damaging issues in their background. Most defense lawyers will bring those up and defuse them before the prosecutor. If the prosecutor gets there before the defendant, then it will cause more harm as it will appear the defendant was hiding the information.

I like to use this tactic when making a cloud-computing sales pitch. When I get to the presentation portion of the pitch, I will then say, "You have probably heard that the cloud is slow, not secure, and expensive." Then I explain what caused those negative perceptions (inexperienced contractors botched many cloud migrations) and point out what has changed (the technology has improved by leaps and bounds).

It's a sign of strength if you bring up those negatives first because it will add to your credibility.

Next, I suggest you focus first and foremost on the time savings features because of the specific job functions that the prospect won't have to perform any longer. Also, don't forget to remind them of the "opportunity cost" savings, which allow employees to exchange wasted time with more productive tasks that will dramatically impact the bottom line. When your service or product will allow the company to have greater control or the ability to accomplish things they couldn't before, then it's best to use real-life scenarios that allow the contact to visualize these benefits. Obviously, if your proposed service/product can potentially increase their profits, then never hesitate to lead off with this aspect. In addition, you can bring up features that will either reduce risk or provide faster service.

Finally, it's appropriate to mention any cost-saving benefits. I always save this for last because having a cold caller tell a business owner they can save them money is a total cliché. When you get to this part of the presentation and deliver this message, though, make sure you both believe in what you're saying and are passionate about it. In the end, your personal belief and passion can be even more persuasive than the features you're explaining.

## The End Game (Closing)

Earlier I mentioned how you can transform the "send information" objection into a windfall of appointments once you figure out how to razzle-dazzle the prospect with an amazing rebuttal. I also alluded to how important it is to anticipate these objections, so you can bring them up before the prospect does and defuse them in advance.

But what if you combine these two ideas by actually bringing up the notion of sending information first and leading the prospect to agree that getting more information would be a good idea? This approach will completely disarm these executives by taking away their objection and using it to force them to agree with you.

You can accomplish all this at the end of your middle game presentation by asking a rhetorical question that assumes the prospect would like to get more information! And this will set you up for the end game portion of the sales pitch, where you begin your drive toward the close.

Once you kick off the end game, it's common for the prospect to start getting nervous and feel the pressure building. This is when you can utilize distraction, like a magician employing sleight of hand.

The most effective way to distract executives is by asking them if they have taken their vacation or travel extensively for work. Feel free to engage in a nice discussion about the details, and if you find out that they do travel for work, ask them where they plan on going next. This technique will move the conversation toward discussing the prospects' calendar while simultaneously building rapport as they talk about themselves.

Once you are certain the prospect's mind is off the

inevitable close, you can transition the call back on track by asking if the prospect has their calendar open. This is a very subtle and subliminal way of getting the prospect thinking about setting a meeting.

This will pave the way toward implementing the strategy I like to call the educational campaign. This is when you convey to the prospect that while you know they are completely happy right now and not looking to change their vendor, your goal is to get the information in their hands so they can be prepared for the future.

Your entire goal at this time is merely to get the best information in their hands, so once they understand all the features, benefits, and pricing, they can make a comparison and clearly comprehend the difference the paradigm shift could make in their business. But there is another goal at play here as well. This is your opportunity to use magical sleight of hand to redefine the phrase: get more information.

Up until this point, the prospect has been interpreting that statement to mean you will just be sending some educational materials in the mail, but there are lots of ways you can get information to an executive besides mailing it or sending an e-mail. The best way is to send a sales representative to make an introduction. And to pull this off, I recommend using a little bait and switch.

The way you do this is to employ the strategy of making the hard thing fun described in Dale Carnegie's How to Win Friends and Influence People. Instead of wasting their time with a typical sales presentation, something most business leaders dread as much as being audited by the IRS, my favorite method is to offer a lunch meeting. Everybody loves a free lunch, especially when you start discussing the type of lunch you're going to bring!

Let me back up a little bit here. You'll want to introduce the idea of a lunch meeting in a nonchalant way. Ask the prospect if they normally eat lunch at their desk or go out for lunch. Often, you will hear from these overworked executives that they are too busy for a formal lunch and have to eat at their desk. Here is where you hook them with a negotiation on what type of food they would enjoy if you stopped by and provided lunch during a brief presentation.

That is when you reveal that you're talking about a visit by the sales rep, but you don't want to focus on that for very long. Instead, switch back to closing on what you will bring for lunch. They will be savvy enough at this point to know what you're talking about, but by offering lunch, you make it a lot easier for them to say yes. I feel this plan of action is probably one of the best ways to make an assumptive close for a face-to-face business meeting.

Don't start celebrating yet, though. You still need to a set date and time for the appointment. The key to this is to focus on tantalizing them with culinary delights. I like to ask them straight out what their favorite restaurant is or their favorite lunch menu. Of course, when you are selling, you never wait around for the prospect to come up with the location or food choices because you should always take the lead. I like to whet the prospect's appetite by mentioning some great local restaurants and throwing out some great take-out options like pizza, BBQ, sandwiches, seafood, or Italian.

Now that you have given your prospect an array of choices, you can wait and listen for them to indicate what they prefer. When they respond by picking an actual restaurant or indicating the type of food they would appreciate, you have just closed the appointment. All you need to do now is tidy up the details and nail down an exact date and time for the lunch meeting.

If you have done what I instructed earlier at the outset of the close, the prospect should already have their calendar open. Now you simply ask them to look at their calendar again to check how the rest of the month looks. I like to phrase the question by saying, "If you were going to have a lunch meeting this month, what day would be the best?" You shouldn't be shocked when, after waiting a few moments, they come back and name a day. Then you just need to check and find out when they normally have lunch and restate the date and time.

Wrap it up like this: "So let's say that our rep stops by [name the day they indicated] on your lunch break at [name the correct hour], and we will bring [name the food option]. Is that okay?" Then transition away from this soft close and inquire how many people will be joining the meeting. This last detail can save the sales rep a lot of embarrassment when he shows up with only two lunches, and there is a room full of other hungry executives expecting to be fed. The worst thing you can possibly do is show up for a meeting without any food when the contact was waiting for you to bring them lunch. So be prepared!

Now all you need to do is input the appointment in the CRM and make sure you have the exact date and time correct, along with any important details like the name of the restaurant or what food to bring and for how many people. Also, you should note exactly which feature/benefit piqued their interest most. This should be added to your notes so the salesperson can review the information before heading to the appointment.

Now celebrate, take a break, ring a bell, and pump your fist! But don't overdo it as this can rub others the wrong way and create some negative blowback.

Closing might sound pretty straight forward, but keep in mind that along the way you can expect to have to handle a few objections. We will discuss objections at length in the next chapter.

Chapter 12

# OVERCOMING OBJECTIONS

Before we discuss practical techniques for overcoming objections, we need to first address your attitude toward objections in general.

When I started out in phone sales and appointment setting, I would cringe when prospects raised the send information objection. I even argued with these C-level decision makers, telling them why it wasn't in my interest to send out printed materials when, in reality, they just didn't want a salesperson visiting their office. Later I realized that by reacting this way, I was sending both direct and indirect signals to the contact that I was displeased with their response.

I didn't understand their objections were actually buying signs I should get excited about.

When you get excited about a contact's objection, you will catch them by surprise because they have probably grown accustomed to cold callers arguing with them instead of listening and eagerly addressing their concerns. So you should adjust your attitude and start thinking about how you can agree with their position without deteriorating your own pitch.

If you want to properly find agreement with the contact, then it's critical you ask the most powerful sales question ever created, the simple question, "Why?" People love to talk about themselves, and when they answer this question, they are essentially giving away the ammunition that will ultimately allow you to craft a successful rebuttal.

I learned the power of this question when I was still in my early childhood. When my dad told my older brother and me we couldn't do something, my brother would count on me to represent us to our parents and convince our father to capitulate.

My entire strategy was based on asking my father why he didn't want to give us permission. When he answered, I would demonstrate my understanding of his concerns then counter by reducing his arguments to absurdity point-by-point. I was so unrelenting that many times my father would in fact reverse his decision. This became an ingrained habit I incorporated into my selling approach.

You see, one of a human being's most powerful desires,

other than feeling important, is to feel understood. This strong desire stems from the extreme lack of people in the world who will truly listen and try to be understanding. Most people we speak with at any length will spend most of their time in the conversation just thinking about what they will say next and not listening. Stephen Covey talks about this in his iconic book, The 7 Habits of Highly Successful People.

If you ask "Why?" with all the prospects who object, you demonstrate you are truly seeking to understand, and this will have a deeply profound effect on them. This is one of the major puzzle pieces I discovered on my quest to set fifteen solid business appointments a day. I can assure you, if you adopt this strategy, it will be a game changer for your cold-calling efforts.

Now that the prospect has revealed why they raised a specific objection, you should find some common ground that will allow you to agree with their position. This is a difficult concept for many people to grasp. "Agree with an objection?! What do you mean?" I often encountered this confusion with the employees who worked at my call center. I can clearly remember one young lady asking me how we can agree with prospects who are arguing with the key points of our presentation. She was assuming that agreeing with the prospect meant she was destroying her position and essentially accepting defeat. But I can assure you that when agreeing, you are not raising the white flag of surrender. Quite the opposite. I will break this technique into pieces so you know what I mean. First, you should not agree with the prospect on substantial differences but instead with the feelings behind their objections. The basic idea is that when an executive cites the reasons behind their objection, they are relating a personal experience and essentially telling you how they feel about what shaped their attitude. Therefore, the way you can agree with the contact's central points of contention is by telling yourself that, if you walked in their shoes and went through the same experience, then most likely you would feel the exact same way as your prospect.

You could also tell yourself that, if you had access to the information or lack thereof, you might also arrive at their same conclusions. You can frame your agreement by saying something along the lines of "If that happened to me, I would feel the same way as you." Or if you have a contentious prospect who adamantly repeats they're happy with what they have, you might say, "It's great your company spent the time to research multiple vendors, ran them through the proper due diligence, and are getting the exact level of service you were promised. I'm sure you're extremely happy and not looking to change, right?"

This technique is what I like to call "aggressively agreeing:" taking the prospect's position and advocating their perspective more passionately than even they would.

You can change the momentum from aggressively agreeing by switching gears and asking a probing question: "When was the last time you did a comparison?" Instead of giving up ground by acquiescing, what you're doing is changing the dynamics so you are no longer in a battle with the prospect but now seen as an unbiased counselor. This approach can soften the most belligerent of opponents because it's hard to resist listening to someone who is on your side. You might be shocked to find that a business leader might even reverse himself and actually advocate for your new position. This is what happens when you make a habit of doing the exact opposite of what people expect.

### The Million-Dollar Rebuttal ("Send Information")

Let's apply the principles we covered in this section to the critical "send information" objection.

You can count on the send information objection to be your absolute number one obstacle. However, if you have laid the proper foundation with your middle game presentation, you can prevail. The first step is to check your attitude by remembering that this objection is really a buying sign and, if handled properly, will result in a booked appointment or sale.

As I mentioned earlier, it's important to get excited in a demonstrable way, so the contact realizes you are going to take their request seriously! I like to say, "I would love to send you some information," and then pause to hear their response. Normally, they will be shocked that a telemarketer is really listening to them and enthusiastically agreeing to what is essentially them blowing you off. There might be a long pause as they regroup. That's where you jump in to continue with your smooth rebuttal.

First, to solidify that you really are serious about sending out whatever information they want, you can ask, "What type of information would you like me to send?" Now you have them on the ropes as they think about what materials they would like. This is where you can take control by throwing out a few suggestions.

The first thing I ask is if they would like to look at some of our references. Then I throw out some red meat containing a trap I know they will almost always fall for: "Would you like to see some numbers?"

Nearly every businessperson would like to get the prices for a product or service before they have to sit through a tedious sales presentation, and sales people instinctively know if they acquiesce, it will kill any chance of getting an appointment. When you give a prospect ballpark figures over the phone, it kills the curiosity you have been building up all throughout the presentation. So why on earth would you offer to throw out numbers to the prospect before you have secured a face-to-face meeting? Because for them it is irresistible. They will feel like they are getting away with something they normally can't with a salesperson, and that leaves them open to your next move: walking it back.

The truth is you should have no intention to ever give out numbers to prospects over the phone because, as we just discussed, it will almost certainly kill the opportunity. But by going along with this request, you can buy some time, and then the goal is to slowly ask enough questions that will reduce the idea of getting numbers to an absurdity in the mind of the executive.

At the beginning, it's a good idea to allow them to feel you're still following through by saying, "I agree that getting numbers is important. However, wouldn't you agree that your business is unique? If we did send some numbers without having a representative make an evaluation of your specific needs, then most likely the proposal will either be too high or too low. You want accurate numbers, correct?"

This is when I like to make the big transition to talking them completely out of the idea of getting information or numbers. I kick this off by making a very bold statement: "I think we might have put the cart before the horse because you might not even want a proposal after hearing a presentation and might not even want to do business with our company. Would I be correct in assuming you only do business with companies you trust regardless of the price? In order to save you time, I suggest we send our salesman over briefly so you can meet the person who represents our company. You can decide very quickly if you trust our company based on how you judge our representative. If you like him and see a possibility of doing business with our company, then he can make a brief presentation, and you can decide based on the details if you even want a proposal, and if then you still want to get some numbers, then at that point, our rep will have gotten all the information we need to give you an accurate estimate. Can I ask you a favor? As long as our rep keeps it brief and is there just to make an introduction, could we meet on [propose a specific date and time]?"

### "You Will Need to Speak with Someone Else"

Another common challenge is when, after you have successfully given a middle game presentation, the C-level decision maker offers to transfer your call to someone else in the company (i.e., passes the buck). Sometimes, inexperienced reps will get fooled by this tactic. Don't.

Remember, a bird in hand is always worth more than two in the bush! Ultimately, the financial executive is often the one you would prefer to meet with because, in most cases, they are higher up in the decision-making process than managers. So if you have that C-level executive on the phone, this is the real opportunity, and you should capitalize on it. Also, if you are transferred, there is no guarantee the other contact will ever pick up. In fact, nine times out of ten, you will end up just getting a voice mail.

It's extremely helpful to look at the situation from their point of view because upper-level management likes to delegate. Businesses seek managers who are highly skilled at delegation. So it's no wonder a senior manager would naturally seek to delegate your call to a lower supervisor who is "in charge of that."

This is when you challenge them by tapping into their pride.

After the senior executive has requested you speak with the manager, you can say, "Great, I would love to speak with your manager. I assume they are more of an expert on that topic." Then I ask the million-dollar question, "Let me ask, are you involved in this decision at all?"

You see, even though company leaders like to delegate, they never want to admit they are not in charge of the final decision. By appealing to their pride, we can trap them into admitting that, in reality, they are the ones we should meet with because they are the real decision makers. That's when I proceed to downplay the nature of the meeting by saying, "The reason I ask is because our first introductory meeting is mainly just about looking at costs versus benefits. We don't get into a lot of technical talk."

I will continue this line of reasoning by saying, "Many times we meet with the financial officer first to make sure there is a real benefit for your company from a financial point of view."

Now you can transition to a closing posture by asking, "Let me ask you for a favor. If we promise not to get too technical and focus on the numbers, could we meet with you first?"

Using this technique will allow you to get more meetings with the C-level person without upsetting them and leave the door open for you to call the manager if you're rejected.

### "Bad Timing: Call Me Back"

There is a popular saying in sales: On every call, a sale is made. Either you sell the prospect on what you're proposing or they sell you on why they can't do it. This saying couldn't be truer than when you have a C-level decision maker trying to

## The Million-Dollar Rebuttal

evade setting an appointment. And a common objection is that it is not the right time.

This is their attempt to sell you on the idea of getting excited about calling them back sometime in the future. The prospect is trying to convince you they are so interested, they will literally be waiting around for you to call them back and set up the meeting.

But your goal as a salesperson is to get people to take action now and see the urgency of not procrastinating. However, you can't go directly at them with that argument because the prospect would merely dig themselves into an intractable position. The proper way forward is to once again agree with them and get excited about the notion of calling them back in the future.

Normally, if they have suggested a fairly reasonable time frame like a few months down the road, I will even say, "That is our exact window as we would like to have a proposal in front of you by that time. You see, our sales process takes about three to six months [depending on what they have said], so if you're going to be ready to review our proposal in a few months, we would've probably needed to start the process much earlier."

The key to this approach lies with impressing upon the prospect that your sales process has such a lengthy lag time that, if postponed, it could cause your company to exceed the time frame they established for reviewing a proposal. Now you can address beginning the sales process earlier.

You can suggest the executive merely get the ball rolling with a brief introductory meeting. I like to explain that, in this phase of the sales cycle, the representative can't even try to make a sale as the meeting is merely introductory in nature. This first step allows the corporate officers to confirm they indeed want to get a proposal in the future when they have time to make an evaluation.

In addition, you can say, "The representative [not a salesman] will be able to collect the information needed for us to begin working on a proposal so we can have it ready in a few months, just when you said you wanted to start making a review." Here we are reminding the prospect that we are looking at the situation from their point of view. We can reinforce this by emphasizing the minimum time requirement needed for the introductory meeting, telling them that the first step of getting some numbers usually only takes about twenty to thirty minutes, unless they have more questions.

Don't lie and say the meeting will just take ten to fifteen minutes. These, decision makers will recognize you're lying, and you will lose the opportunity up front, or the salesman will walk into an ambush later. Ultimately, your objective should be to get the prospect to visualize the time lag in such a way that they realize delaying the process by two or three months will cause them to dramatically overshoot their time horizon for due diligence by as much as six more months to a year.

Though you want to create a sense of urgency, be aware of the terminology you use. You will want to employ more positive terminology as negative terms will induce a feeling of commitment from a prospect, which could cause them to reject your proposition. That's why in the above rebuttal, we suggested calling the first meeting, not a sales meeting, but an "introductory meeting" where we are just picking up information.

In the credit card game, the objection we encountered most often was consumers telling us they didn't want the bank to send out a physical credit card. For them, this implied they had made a commitment to use the credit card.

The way most calling agents would deal with this objection was by telling the prospect, "All we ask is that you delay your final decision until you have a chance to try out all the benefits. After all, you can cancel the card at any time." This idea of delaying their final decision had a very powerful effect on consumers as it relieved them of the feeling of commitment and being locked into a decision.

The bottom line, when you're addressing the call-back objection, is you want to use language that invokes the feeling of choice instead of commitment. You never want to speak about a sales meeting or even call the representative a salesperson. Meanwhile you want to convince the procrastinators that postponing the review process will just cause the process to take longer and get that much more complicated.

As long as you faithfully employ positive phrasing in your sales language and can get procrastinators to visualize how getting started earlier will allow them to meet their own time tables, you will be the one on the call making the sale instead of the prospect selling you.

Chapter 13

# HOW TO MAKE CALLBACKS

Unfortunately, even the best strategies won't convince all the procrastinators all the time. Inevitably, you will have to put one of these executives on your callback list.

In this case, here is some sage advice that will save you from falling into an eternal cycle of call backs and dead ends where you call the prospect only to hear, "Call me back in a few more weeks."—a situation I've experienced more times than I would like to reveal.

The last time I got stuck in this callback hell, I had an executive tell me to call him back at least ten different times before I got completely fed up and had to remind myself of the definition of insanity: doing exactly the same thing and expecting different results. This is when I decided to take a 180-degree shift by putting a new practice in place.

I knew I wasn't going to call a prospect back and then remind them that they had already told me to call them back before I asked if they were ready to book their appointment. I had already tried that, and it never worked. Therefore, when I called the prospect back, I promised myself that, no matter what, I wouldn't discuss why I had called back or what I wanted. In other words, I was determined to call and discuss everything under the sun (the stock market, sports, weather, business, and even politics), so long as I didn't mention that I was calling them back.

As I was implementing this new strategy, something very strange happened. After I had gotten his opinion on his favorite sports team, asked if he followed the market, and inquired about why he started his business, he abruptly stopped me and said, "Weren't you the gentleman calling me to discuss employee leasing?" I said yes and listened as he opened up his calendar. Then after what seemed like an eternity of silence, he came back on the line and indicated a definite date when our rep could visit him to discuss the matter.

Eureka! After calling this procrastinating executive back literally dozens of times, I had finally hit pay dirt! I was still in shock as I got off the phone and inputted all the appointment information in the CRM. I just couldn't figure out what had happened. Then it dawned on me that I has just discovered how to implement one of the famous principles Carnegie advocates in *How to Win Friends and Influence People*.

The ultimate way to persuade someone to adopt your point of view is by letting the other person think the idea is theirs. I had known about this amazing concept, but trying to discover a process to implement the principle had evaded me for years. That's when I made it my policy never to bring up what I wanted on callbacks and leave it to the client to do so.

Of course, the objective should always be to book appointments the first time you reach an executive, but if you must call them back, this is a solid strategy that will bring you surprising results.

Chapter 14

# USING EMOTION EFFECTIVELY

I was first alerted to the strength of getting emotional with qualified candidates during a sales meeting at a law firm. An employee and I were meeting with an office manager to sell managed services by focusing on her weak data backup system. In this situation, the office manager had already agreed that her company's network was unstable and likely to crash. That was when my associate asked one of the most penetrating questions I have ever heard.

He asked her, "If your network crashed and the backup system failed, leading to massive downtime, then how would that personally affect you?" As soon as he asked this question, you could literally see her wheels turning. Then she responded, "I would probably be fired since it's my responsibility!" She was so motivated that we got the contract signed within a week of the initial sales meeting.

When I reflected on that question, I realized that the magic hinged on the last portion: "how would this *personally* affect you?" The phrasing reminded me of one of the best sales pitches I had ever made when I worked at MBNA America. I had gotten in contact with a woman who had been preapproved for a Gold MasterCard, but she objected to getting the card because she said her husband had plenty of credit cards already and didn't need another. This is a fairly common objection when you're pitching credit cards to consumers with good credit.

Instead of using my usual rebuttal, I zeroed in on the fact that she had said her husband had plenty of credit cards. This is when I took the call into the emotional realm by asking her point-blank if she had any credit cards in her own name. When she honestly responded that she didn't, I followed up with, "I don't want to get negative, but I believe it's good to be prepared," and she agreed.

So I continued, "Don't get me wrong. I hope your marriage lasts, but the divorce rate is over 50 percent. I have heard horror stories of women who didn't have their own credit and had a difficult time after a divorce. Don't you think it would be a good idea to at least have one credit card in your name, so you can start building credit?" I followed this by reminding her she was already pre-approved. I was able to get the entire credit application filled out, and I honestly believe the consumer was happy I took a moment to reason with her on an emotional level.

None of that was intentional. At the time, I just stumbled upon the tactic, and it would be almost another twenty years before it would dawn on me to start using emotion in a systematic way. I learned that, by asking how having, or not having, a feature or benefit would affect a prospect personally, I can make a huge difference in the outcome of a call.

You will know you've successfully influenced your target on a personal level when they stop talking about their work life and start talking about their family life. If a prospect connects to your message on a personal level, you might hear them say things like, "I will have more time to spend with my kids," "I can save my marriage," "I will actually be able to take a vacation for the first time," etc. If you can remember to always incorporate the personal appeal in your presentation, you will find prospects extremely motivated as they will not easily forget your conversation.

If you want to really hone your skill at employing the powerful art of the emotional approach in your sales presentation, then I highly recommend reading *Switch* by Chip and Dan Heath.

Chapter 15

# A WORD OF CAUTION

I want to share with you an experience I had while training a couple of IT salespeople at a large technology firm in Pennsylvania.

The company had purchased some training materials from me a few months earlier and had just accepted my invitation to conduct some on-site sales training for their two salespeople. When I arrived at their offices, I was greeted by one of the salespeople I had spoken to over the phone during some of my training calls. This gentleman was recruited by the technology firm from the mortgage industry after the Great Recession in 2008 and, with the use of my training materials, had become a self-sufficient appointment setter who was closing his own deals.

I spent some time in his office listening to him make some cold calls when he hit pay dirt on setting an appointment. What I found so amazing about listening to him was that it seemed like I was listening to a recording of one of my own cold calls. Later when I accompanied him on a couple of sales calls, I observed that he was using all my sales techniques verbatim as well, and to great effect.

You see, he had studied my materials and videos and had adopted my entire system! This was so exciting because so often the human element rears its ugly head, and your average person will seek to change up the pitch and rebuttals to make it their own. This usually destroys all the benefits of my system.

Later I met with the manager and the other employee they were training to be a dedicated cold caller. After we sat down, I asked to see the materials they were using to train this employee and was shocked to see my materials literally jumbled up and edited beyond imagination. Immediately, I could see the problem. The manager had attempted to make my training materials her own and was training the new employee with an ineffective system.

This new telemarketer didn't make it for very long; however, the young man who had copied my training so closely continued to be successful and was eventually recruited to be the sales director for another large IT firm.

I say this not to gloat but just as a word of caution that you should take the materials and implement them as they are constructed, and resist the urge to alter them dramatically. Of course I encourage you to utilize the principles I have laid out, like aggressively agreeing, and apply them to create your own rebuttals, but when you take what I have provided at face value and use it in the method I have suggested, then the only limit to what you can achieve lies in your own imagination!

Chapter 16

# MY TWO CENTS ON IMPLEMENTATION

Over the years, I have run into many business owners who said they tried cold calling but failed, and they no longer believe it to be a viable marketing strategy. Never mind that at the same time, our call center was able to generate millions of dollars in revenue for other companies through our appointment-setting services. The truth is that cold calling only works when you have all the right components and they all come into alignment.

First and foremost, the services you're calling about have to have an edge in the marketplace—one that you can educate prospects about. Then you need to have the right calling strategy along with a motivated salesperson to make those calls. Lastly, you will need a salesperson who is not simply an order taker but has true teaching abilities that allow them to light a fire under even lukewarm prospects, spurring them to take action.

If you happen to be the salesperson who's going to make your own calls, then you don't have to worry about the salesperson 'burning' the leads since you have confidence in your own abilities. However, if your company has enacted division of labor by hiring both a cold caller and a salesperson, then you will have to be very cautious of the dynamics between these two divisions. Often I have seen a great cold-calling campaign go down in flames because the salesperson lacked fundamental skills.

However, sometimes the cold callers are not motivated and incentivized correctly, so they can also sabotage the success of the overall marketing campaign. But often the cause of a cold caller dropping the ball has more to do with the environment they work in than their skills.

Telemarketing is often viewed as a second-rate job, but the pay scale often compounds that negative view of the position. As a result of that stigma, the hiring net usually ends up bringing in the bottom of the barrel in terms of personnel. This scenario often becomes a self-fulfilling prophecy as the campaign ends up failing because you have the wrong people involved in the first place.

If you have read my materials, then you should agree with me that anyone that can master my practices is nothing less than a salesperson! This means that the people you should be looking for are in fact highly skilled individuals who have the same attributes as the salespeople in the field. However, you're never going to attract the right people to work for your company until you change how the cold-calling position is viewed and make the employment package more attractive.

When I follow up with cold-calling naysayers, it usually turns out they were paying their people peanuts and expecting miracles! One of the lessons I have learned over the years is that if you expect something amazing to happen, then you should plant amazing seeds.

Finally, it's important that you have a manager who is not on the cold-calling team or on the sales team but one who is actually going out to randomly verify that the appointments being set are in fact quality leads based on the company's criteria. This way you are not relying on the sales people who have their own agenda to be the sole judge of the cold-calling team's success.

In closing, I hope you or your company can harness my materials in such an amazing way that your cold-calling campaigns surpass any of my accomplishments! In the words of Blake from *Glengarry Glen Ross*, "Go and do likewise, gents."

# WANT DAVID TO TRAIN YOUR STAFF?

David Walter works with corporations & entrepreneurs who want to implement his lead generation secrets to achieve stratospheric success by getting their staff into the zone and teaching his counterintuitive scripts along with the million dollar rebuttal!

**CONNECT WITH DAVID**
Matthew Raggo - Training Coordinator for David Walter
210.764.4080
david@stratosphericleadgenerationsecrets.com
StratosphericLeadGenerationSecrets.com/Speaking

# BOOKS THAT INFLUENCED ME & I RECOMMEND:

- *The 10X Rule* by Grant Cardone
- *Outliers* by Malcolm Gladwell
- *Good to Great* by Jim Collins
- *See You at the Top* by Zig Ziglar
- *Awaken the Giant Within* by Tony Robbins
- *Think and Grow Rich* by Napoleon Hill
- *The Pumpkin Plan* by Mike Michalowicz
- *The Pursuit of Happiness* by Chris Gardner
- *How to Win Friends and Influence People* by Dale Carnegie
- *Switch* by Dan Heath
- *Start With Why* – How Great Leaders Inspire Everyone to Take Action by Simon Sinek
- *The Wealth of Nations* by Adam Smith
- *The Breakthrough Company* by Keith McFarland

- *The 4-Hour Work Week* by Tim Ferris
- *The Power of Focus: What the World's Greatest Achievers Know About the Secret to Financial Freedom & Success* by Jack Canfield, Mark Victor Hansen, & Les Hewitt
- *High Profit Prospecting* by Mark Hunter
- *The 7 Habits of Highly Effective People* – Dr. Stephen R. Covey
- *Grow Rich While You Sleep* – Ben Sweetland
- *You Don't Have to be a Shark – Creating Your Own Success* by Robert Herjavec
- *Believe it to Achieve It: Overcome Your Doubts, Let Go of Your Past, and Unlock Your True Potential* by Brian Tracy

# WANT DAVID TO SPEAK AT YOUR NEXT EVENT?

David loves to get audiences fired up about about getting in the zone to accomplish amazing uncanny business feats, like he did with his 'million dollar rebuttal'

We can work with meeting planners to customize our presentations to fit your needs or audience.

## CONNECT WITH DAVID

Matthew Raggo - Speaking Coordinator for David Walter
210.764.4080
david@stratosphericleadgenerationsecrets.com
StratosphericLeadGenerationSecrets.com/Speaking

## DAVID RECOMMENDS:

### ZoomInfo

I recommend ZoomInfo to get contact lists that are more accurate and have more names of decision makers, saving you time during your lead qualifying process.

www.zoominfo.com
866-904-9666

### Salesforce

I recommend Salesforce because it's the most universally used CRM, which means it integrates into everything, it's cloud-based so you can get it up and running quickly, and it has modules with additional features to increase productivity.

www.salesforce.com
888-747-9736

## IT Vendors:

Here are some additional services that can help IT companies change their model and become the message leader:

## IT Trade Shows:

Here are some trade shows that you should attend to learn about new services that could be your new message leaders!

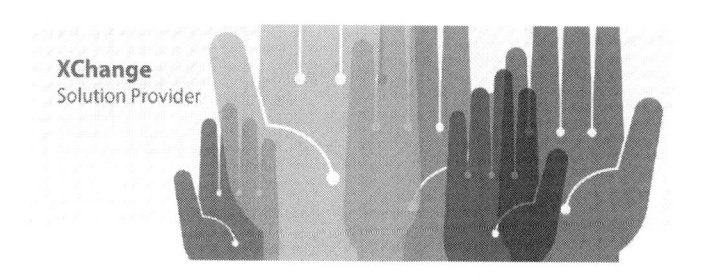

**The ChannelPro Network**

**XChange Solution Provider**

**CompTIA ChannelCon**

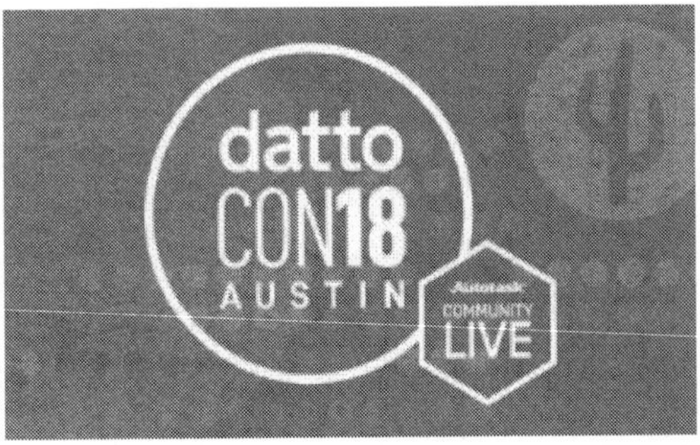
datto
CON18
AUSTIN
COMMUNITY
LIVE

Printed in Great Britain
by Amazon